Great Session Openers, Closers, and Energizers

Great Session Openers, Closers, and Energizers

Quick Activities for Warming Up Your Audience and Ending on a High Note

Marlene Caroselli

McGraw-Hill
New York   San Francisco   Washington, D.C.   Auckland   Bogotá
Caracas   Lisbon   London   Madrid   Mexico City   Milan
Montreal   New Delhi   San Juan   Singapore
Sydney   Tokyo   Toronto

Library of Congress Cataloging-in-Publication Data

Caroselli, Marlene
    Great openers, closers, and energizers : 101 quick activities for
warming up your audience and ending on a high note / Marlene
Caroselli.
        p.   cm.
        ISBN 0-07-012009-9 (looseleaf). — ISBN 0-07-012010-2 (pbk.)
        1. Employees–Training of.   2. Training.   3. Group games.
    I. Title.
HF5549.5.T7C298513   1998
658.3'124—dc21   97-48489
                                                    CIP

McGraw-Hill

A Division of The McGraw·Hill Companies

Permission is granted free of charge to photocopy the pages of this training book which are required for use by participants attending a training workshop. Only an original purchaser conducting training sessions may make such photocopies. Under no circumstance is it permitted to sell or distribute on a commercial basis material reproduced from this publication. Except as expressly provided above, no part of this book may be reproduced or distributed in any form or by any means, or stored in a database or retrieval system, without the prior written permission of the publisher. Permission may be obtained by contacting

The McGraw-Hill Companies
Permissions Department, 13th Floor
1221 Avenue of the Americas
New York, NY 10020, U.S.A.

Telephone: 212-512-2574
Fax: 212-512-6285

5 6 7 8 9 0 EDW / EDW 0 5 4 3 2 1   **(Looseleaf)**
12 13 14 EDW / EDW 0 9 8 7 6 5   **(Paperback)**

ISBN 0-07-012010-2 [paperback]
PN 0-07-012051-X
PART OF
ISBN 0-07-012009-9 [looseleaf]

The sponsoring editor for this book was Richard Narramore, the editing supervisor was Fred Dahl, and the production supervisor was Pamela Pelton. It was set in Futura Light by Inkwell Publishing Services.

Printed and bound by Edwards Brothers, Inc.

 This book is printed on recycled, acid-free paper containing a minimum of 50% recycled de-inked fiber.

McGraw-Hill books are available at special quantity discounts to use as premiums and sales promotions, or for use in corporate training programs. For more information, please write to the Director of Special Sales, McGraw-Hill, 11 West 19th Street, New York, NY 10011. Or contact your local bookstore.

CONTENTS

INTRODUCTION

No matter what training you may be conducting, no matter what session you may be facilitating, you will find these openers, closers, and energizers applicable to the material you are using. The activities in this book are flexible enough to accommodate a few or many minutes' worth of time and curricular space. Many can be expanded from filler status to concept status, thus helping you communicate the main points of your presentation. Recognizing that exemplary trainers are constantly renewing themselves and the material they present, *Great Session Openers, Closers, and Energizers* will help you put a new face on the core body of knowledge you possess. The activities are adaptable to any instructional setting; the applications made smoother via what I call "transition tag lines." These unique segues allow you to provide a seamless connection between these stimulating, fun-oriented exercises and the instructional content you are presenting.

These are dynamic activities, but by no means are they all fun and games. Just the opposite, in fact. These openers, closers, and energizers are designed to help you achieve your instructional objectives. They are ready-to-use learning exercises, transferable to any discipline and adaptable to any employment setting following the training. Their flexibility allows you to tailor them to meet your presenting and training needs. You will find, combining the exercises themselves, the follow-up ideas, and the transitional suggestions, hundreds of ways to add value to the content you are emphasizing and the context within which it is presented.

FORMAT OF THE BOOK

Great Session Openers, Closers, and Energizers is divided into three sections, each of which contains over 30 activities. Handouts or transparencies needed for the activity appear at the end of each exercise. Often competitive in nature, these activities challenge participants to combine their collective talents to solve problems, make decisions, answer questions, create new knowledge, and synthesize their thoughts. In so doing, participants interact in ways that make learning more enjoyable. "What we learn with pleasure," Alfred Mercier asserts, "we never forget."

Openers

The opening moments of a training program set the stage for the subsequent script to be enacted. If comfort zones are established early, if challenges are positively presented, if overviews are clear, and if participants are stimulated to contribute, then the opening and closing acts, as well as the main event, should be well-received. The openers in this portion of the book will help you start every session on the right foot.

For the most part, these openers are brief interactions that help set the tone for the instructional modules to follow. They encourage participants to learn more about you, about their fellow participants, and about themselves. Additionally, they help create a climate within which you can do your best teaching and participants can do their best learning. These starters send the message that participation is expected and teamwork is valued.

While openers or icebreakers open a training session, many of these can also be used to introduce a large instructional section. They provide a welcome change of pace from the solid lecture blocks that constitute the course content.

Energizers

There are times in the course of a trainer's day when fillers are needed. For example, a major chunk of the instructional day has just been completed and yet there are five minutes left before lunch. Or, it's after lunch, and only three-quarters of the class has returned. You want to get started, but you don't want to get into the next major portion of the curriculum without having the whole class present. The energizers will help you pique interest in the next informational segment so you can start the afternoon session on time and yet avoid having to play catch-up for latecomers.

No matter how inspiring or skilled the instructor, lessons invariably lag at some point, for example, during the energy sap that occurs shortly after the noon hour. Use these energizers for just such occasions. They are inspiring and can help you segue into the subsequent content.

Closers

Sometimes the excellence of a training session is diluted by a lack of appropriate closure. This time period represents the instructor's final opportunity to summarize the key points of the preceding lectures and activities, the last chance to point participants in the direction of future success. And yet, many instructors fail to take advantage of these final moments. In this section you'll find 33 activities designed to lend instructional panache and pizzazz to the ends of classes.

These activities represent your final opportunity to restate the objectives of the course, to stress again the key concepts in the instructional outline, to intensify the learning experience, and to urge participants to put theories into practice. Use the closers here to motivate participants to transfer learning to their particular job situations.

For your convenience, the following matrix categorizes these 100 exercises by time. The length of each activity is indicated in the left-hand column, immediately after the number of the activity and just before the title. The formations are shown immediately after the title via these initials:

WC = The whole class engages in this activity, usually working individually.

SG = Small groups work best with this activity.

LG = Seven or more participants work as a team on activities marked LG.

P = Partners or pairs will be needed for this activity.

T = Triads participate in this activity together.

Finally, the kind of activity is indicated by a bullet in one of these columns:

Quiz/Assessment = Participants typically work alone on these stimulating prompts, design to elicit introspection.

Mental Challenge = Puzzles, conundrums, and other brainteasers are presented via these stimulating exercises.

Discussion = These thought-provoking exercises are designed to generate the lively exchange of viewpoints either in small groups or with the class as a whole.

Insight/Awareness = Designed to develop awareness of self, others, and issues related to training and business, these exercises call for serious thinking on the part of participants.

Introductory = Participants engage in getting-to-know-you gestures with these introductory exercises.

OPENERS

		Quiz	Challenge	Discussion	Insight/ Awareness	Intro- ductory
1:15 Certainty? Certainly!	WC	•				
2:20 Missing Letters	SG		•			
3:10 What Do You Expect?	SG			•		
4:15 Butterflies in the Buttermilk	SG			•		
5:20 Flubs & Dubs	WC				•	
6:15 I-Openers	T					•
7:15 I'm Not Confused. I'm Just Well-Mixed!	SG		•			
8:05 Initial Inerrogations	P				•	
9:15 Let Me Introduce Myself	SG					•
10:10 Priority Partners	P					•
11:15 When You Ask a Dumb Question	SG				•	
12:20 Square: Won	SG					•
13:15 The Cube of Intellect	SG		•			
14:15 Life Lines	SG				•	
15:05 Matching Wits	T		•			
16:10 Past, Present & Future	SG				•	
17:20 Calling Cards	WC					•
18:05 Don't Have/Don't Want	P					•
19:10 The Dave Clark Five Is Taking Over	SG				•	
20:15 Memories Are Made of This	SG				•	
21:20 Answer Me This	T					•
22:05 Seeing Red, White & Blue	T		•			
23:05 Biz Buz	SG		•			
24:05 Ex Libris	SG		•			
25:15 Smarts à la Will Rogers	SG	•				
26:10 The Choice Is Yours	SG	•				
27:10 Can You Find the Pattern?	SG			•		
28:10 Define and Shine	SG			•		
29:15 Meet Me in the Middle	LG			•		
30:15 A Word From the Wise	SG			•		
31:10 Intuit and Out of It	LG	•				
32:10 Meta4, 4 U	SG			•		
33:10 Raconterse	SG			•		
34:10 Defensive Lines	SG			•		

Note that, for the Energizers, the column previously titled Introductory has been renamed Creative Stimulators. These are truly energizing activities, many of them competitive in nature, that will stimulate creativity and high-energy input.

ENERGIZERS		Quiz	Challenge	Discussion	Insight/ Awareness	Creative-Stimulators
35:05 Tri-Dents	SG		•			
36:10 Forced Fits	SG		•			
37:10 Each One Teach One	P				•	
38:10 And the Paraphrase Goes To…	SG					•
39:15 And the Award Goes To…	SG					•
40:10 M Prompt: U	SG		•			
41:30 That's Debatable	LG			•		
42:05 Paint-the-Trainer	WC					•
43:10 The Sixty-Second Interview	LG		•			
44:15 S-Teams	SG					•
45:10 Delphian Deliberations	WC				•	
46:10 Clipping the Wings of Creativity	LG			•		
47:10 The Big 3	SG	•				
48:30 Panels—Wooden & Otherwise	LG			•		
49:15 The Dashing Young Plan on the Flying Trapeze	SG				•	
50:10 Snurfing USA	SG					•
51:05 Self-Symbols	SG					•
52:15 Running the Course	LG			•		
53:15 From Unknowing to Unknowingly	SG	•				
54:05 There Are Fewer Rules Than You Think	LG					•
55:05 Master Files	SG				•	
56:05 Always Say "Never"	LG				•	
57:05 Exhilarating Disruptions	WC					•
58:05 Alliterative Associations	T		•			
59:10 (Court) Case Study	SG			•		
60:10 It's in the Cards	T					•
61:10 How'm I Doin?	WC			•		
62:30 Centenary Capsules	LG			•		
63:30 Taming the Tension Tyrant	T					•
64:10 If I Were to Ask You	SG	•				
65:15 Are You a "Somebody"?	T			•		
66:05 Eve & Adam Bombs	P				•	
67:30 Gut Responses/ Gutsy Responders	WC	•				

CLOSERS	Quiz	Challenge	Discussion	Insight/ Awareness	Intro-ductory
68:30 Stratified Summaries SG		•			
69:40 Lights, Camera, Fractions SG					•
70:10 Sweet Seventeen LG		•			
71:15 The Ring of Sports SG					•
72:10 Slo-Mo Sow; Grow WC	•				
73:10 Bizarrely Committed SG				•	
74:10 Worst-Case Scenarios SG				•	
75:15 Lessons Learned SG			•		
76:05 Wiggle Giggles WC	•				
77:05 Next Steps WC					•
78:15 Best-in-Class outputs T					•
79:20 Certifiable WC					•
80:15 Designer Gleans P	•				
81:20 Arti-Chokes LG					•
82:10 The Letterman List SG					•
83:20 InternViews LG		•			
84:10 You's for You to Use P				•	
85:10 Sit 'n' Wit WC				•	
86:05 Educational Equations P					•
87:10 Prove It! P					•
88:15 Commencement Seekers T					•
89:15 The Point Is... WC	•				
90:05 Training Bras SG					•
91:05 Friendly Persuasion WC	•				
92:15 Those Who Can... SG				•	
93:10 Plottery Tickets SG					•
94:15 Zip 'n' Tuck SG					•
95:05 Tooth or Consequences SG					•
96:10 Hy-Fun SG		•			
97:15 Presume to Subsume SG				•	
98:15 Juxtaposed Pairs SG					•
99:20 Giving You the Runaround WC	•				
100:15 Sumo Sums SG					•

FORMAT OF THE ACTIVITIES

Form

In the first part of each lesson, you will find the particulars: how much time is needed, how the class should be arranged, the ideal group size, the materials you will need, et cetera.

Function

Each lesson is organized around a familiar approach: a structured practice or role-play exercise, a mini-lecture, an individual assignment, a small-group activity, a team task, or a lecture-with-quiz format. In the Function section, the procedure to follow with the particular approach is sequentially delineated. Sample lectures are often included (in italics). Add to or subtract from the text to make it suitable for your own needs.

Follow-up

This section in each activity recommends ways to continue the learning or skill development. The recommendation may be in the form of a book to be read, a topic to be investigated, an interview to be conducted, or a task to be completed upon return to the workplace. All too often, ideas and insights are born in a classroom only to be allowed to wither and die once the training has been completed. The follow-up activity is designed to move knowledge from its embryonic to its empowering status.

Transition

These suggested statements will help you move smoothly from the opener, energizer, or closer to the logical next step in the session. Without these transitions participants may feel they are jumping from one concept to another with no sense of order or planned sequence.

John Wooden once observed, "It's what you learn after you know it all that counts." By using this collection of session openers, closers, and energizers, you are acknowledging your commitment to continuous learning, to constant upgrading of your professional repertoire. You are also pledging to make "learning" as meaningful as possible for the adult learners whose paths you cross. May your instructional journeys always have excellence as their destination.

OPENERS

1

CERTAINTY? CERTAINLY!

FORM

This activity requires no material beyond the instructor's list of questions plus paper and pencils for participants to answer the questions. Any number of class members can participate in the exercise, which takes approximately 15 minutes, including the discussion.

FUNCTION

Essentially, this activity is a mini-lecture illustrating the importance of being open-minded, particularly in a training session. The lecture further demonstrates the truth of this assertion: "The only people for whom training does not work are those who think they are already perfect."

1.   Begin by saying you have a short quiz for participants to take. Say that, because it is early in the class and you want to boost their self-confidence, you will permit them to give their answer in the form of a range. Sample verbiage follows:

> *If I were to ask you to guess my age, you would have trouble pinpointing it exactly. But if I permitted you to give an answer that fell within a range, you might say, "between thirty and sixty." [Adjust accordingly.] And you would be right. So, for each of these ten questions, write a range, so that you have a 100 percent chance of getting the correct answer. Be realistic—for my age, for example, it would have been foolish to say, "Between 5 and 100." The more realistic answer would have been, "Between 30 and 60." Ready? Number from one to ten.*

2.   Proceed to ask the questions that follow.

> 1.   *The computer can solve the Rubik's Cube puzzle in four minutes. How long did it take the world champion?*
>
> 2.   *Out of one hundred pieces of information we receive, how many do we remember?*
>
> 3.   *In a famous study of creativity, the same students were given the same test at various stages of their lives. At age five, 92 percent of them were deemed "very creative." What was the percentage when they were in college?*

4. How long did the first U.S. satellite stay in space?

5. How much money would you have if you started with a penny and doubled the amount each day for a month?

6. According to Training magazine, what percentage of all U.S. companies have at least some employees working in teams?

7. How many five- and six-letter words can be made from the letters in the word "i n c u b a t e d"?

8. What percentage of purchased vegetables go to waste in the average American household?

9. According to a study by Michael Lewis, professor of pediatrics and psychiatry at the Robert Wood Johnson Medical School, what percentage of children, if any, are telling lies by the time they are two years old?

10. How many pages long is the Oxford English Dictionary?

3. Supply the answers:

1. The world champion was a sixteen-year-old, who assembled the cube in 22.95 seconds.

2. Scientists estimate we only retain one out of one hundred.

3. Only 2 percent of the same students, taking the same test, were deemed "very creative" as college students.

4. The satellite was in space for twelve years, from 1958 to 1970.

5. The penny would become $5,368,709.12!

6. Eighty percent of American employees are working in groups identified as teams.

7. You can actually make 27 five-letter words and 13 six-letter words.

8. As a nation, we waste 32 percent of the vegetables we buy. (The total wasted food in this country would be enough to feed all of Canada, according to a survey in USA Today.)

9. Seventy percent of children are already telling lies by that age.

10. The OED, as it is affectionately called, has 16,400 pages.

4. Continue with the lecture.

Did anyone have a perfect score? [Chances are, no one did. Feign surprise.] *No one? But I gave you enough latitude with the ranges to ensure you would have correct answers!*

Actually, I use this little quiz to remind you that as smart as you are, you do not know everything. Nor do I. In a training session, there is much to be learned—by all of us, from all of us. I hope you will participate fully in this training today, asking questions, sharing experiences, and discussing issues that are relevant. It's fine to be certain about what you know but realize that sometimes that very certitude establishes barriers. Be definite, be assured, but, please, also be open.

FOLLOW-UP

A quizmaster could be appointed to publicly post one question each week, related to the topic of the training or to the industry itself. At the end of a 6-month period, the employee with the most correct (or most nearly correct) answers, would win a token prize. The questions should evoke interesting discussion and should also keep employees apprised of the latest statistics regarding their particular industry.

TRANSITION

For the rest of the day, I hope you will keep an open mind. I hope you will realize that, as certain as you are of the knowledge you possess, that certitude may prevent you from acquiring new knowledge. Be firm in your convictions, yes, but allow yourself to consider viewpoints and assertions that may be at odds with your own points of view.

2
MISSING LETTERS

In advance of the class beginning, identify ten words that will have most relevance for what you will be presenting. Isolate those words and write their letters in pie-slice circles—going either clockwise or counterclockwise. Leave one letter out of each word. Turn the circles so the first letter of the word does not appear at the top of the circle.

For example, for a class on teambuilding, one important word might be *champion*, referring to the member of upper management who serves as coach or advocate for the team.

This word is shown below with the *c* missing, with the *c* not in the top or usual beginning point, and with the spelling moving counterclockwise.

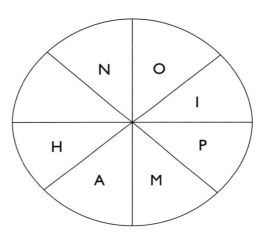

Have the words ready on transparency or chart paper, and allow participants to work in small groups to solve them. In total, the solving of your words and the cohorts' words, along with related discussions, should take 20–30 minutes.

FUNCTION

1. Ask students to form small groups and to figure out ten words that will be presented to them (on the overhead or on flip chart paper).

2. Explain in a mini-lecture:

These words have special relevance for me because they represent the foundation of this course. They are the building blocks that will permit you to develop the mental structures you

14

will need for full understanding of the main points of this training. How quickly can you figure out what these key words are?

3.   The first team to finish is appointed the Carry-On Cohorts. They will prepare a list of ten of their own words in the same way and will use the words as springboards for class discussion. As they prepare the list, other class members can share with one another their own puzzle words created to emphasize instructional points.

FOLLOW-UP

A class scrapbook could be assembled and sent out as advance learning assignments for future class members, who will come to class prepared at the very least with a list of the important instructional elements.

Alternatively, take all the circle words and distribute two to each group. Have groups write a one- or two-sentence response, explaining the importance of each word within the framework of the course content.

If it is possible to assemble the managers who gave permission for these participants to attend (perhaps at a brown-bag luncheon), the students could share their responses to the words they were assigned in an effort to bring the training back to the workplace.

TRANSITION

For the remainder of this session, I'd like you to do two things:

1.   *Keep a list of key words—ones you feel constitute the essence of this training program.*

2.   *Keep a list of missing points. In other words, what did I fail to make clear to you? What did I skip over or skim over? Later this afternoon, we can fill in, not the missing letters, but the pieces of information that you need to make the knowledge picture complete.*

3

WHAT DO YOU EXPECT?

FORM

This simple activity accomplishes a number of goals:

(a) It gets participants thinking about what they intend to put into and take out of this training.

(b) It affords them an opportunity—within the first few minutes of convening—to begin working together.

(c) It provides you the opportunity to correlate your goals for teaching with participants' goals for learning. If a gap appears to exist, you can explain why a particular topic is not included or perhaps can choose to incorporate it into your lesson plans.

Groups work together to determine their learning goals during a 10-minute period. Then, each group appoints a spokesperson to report on their collective responses. They need no materials other than paper and pencils. However, if the lists are put on chart paper, you can allude to them several times during the course of the training session.

FUNCTION

1. This activity requires little by way of introduction. Essentially, you will divide the class into table groups of five or six and ask them to discuss their expectations for the course. If possible, have them write their lists on chart paper.

2. Call on a spokesperson from each team to share their ideas. Comment on each briefly, either affirming its place in your curricular plans or else explaining why a particular expectation cannot be met within the scope of the course content. For those that are repeated by later groups, you need not restate your comments.

3. If the expectations are posted, you can use them at various points during the training to energize the group. You might say, for example, "Let's take a mental break now and review what we have accomplished so far this morning. Would each of you get up, walk around the room, and check off on these lists all the expectations that have been partially or fully met so far?"

Of course, you can do the same thing as a closing activity to demonstrate the extent to which customer satisfaction has been attained.

FOLLOW-UP

By the end of the session, ask each participant to decide which of all the expectations that have been met was most valuable to him or her. Ask each person to share that selection (and an explanation of its importance) with his or her supervisor when he or she returns to work. Or, participants can share their selections with one other employee who may sign up for the same training in the future.

TRANSITION

Now that I have a sense of your expectations for me and for this program, let me share with you my expectations—not only for accomplishing the course objectives but also my expectations for you as absorbers of knowledge.

4

BUTTERFLIES IN THE BUTTERMILK

FORM

Assuming the class can be arranged in table groups, place a quart of buttermilk, paper napkins, and small cups (one per participant) in the center of each table. The entire exercise takes about 15 minutes and is an excellent illustration of the difficulties leaders have in instituting change. (Note: If it is difficult to obtain the buttermilk, any other unusual food or beverage could be used.)

FUNCTION

1.   Make this announcement at the very beginning of the training session, immediately after you have told participants your name and the course title.

> *Before we begin today's training program, I would like to con-duct a simple experiment. First, though, you will need a team leader. Would the person at each table with the longest hair serve in that capacity? [Pause as those people are chosen.] Thank you. Your job today will be to persuade each person at your table to drink a small glass of buttermilk. At each table will be an observer, who will make note of actions, reactions, and interactions.*

Ask one person at each table to observe, recording his or her insights on paper, to be shared later with the entire group.

2.   Allow about 10 minutes and then ask the observers to share what they have observed.

FOLLOW-UP

Encourage participants to keep a log, once the training is complete, of changes that have been presented to them at work. They should also note how well they and others adjusted to the changes.

TRANSITION

> *For many very good reasons, some of you were unwilling to change your basic eating pattern. If it did not include buttermilk before, you were determined that it would not include butter-milk now. Some of you may have had health reasons, like lac-tose intolerance, and so you were adamant about not chang-ing. Others may have found "butterflies" swarming in your stomachs at the very thought of doing something new and dif-ferent. Others were hesitant, waiting to see how your col-*

leagues reacted before trying the change yourselves. Still others demonstrated the devil-may-care, I'll-try-anything-once attitudes that characterize extreme risk takers.

Your reactions to the buttermilk experiment actually parallel normal reactions to new experiences, new knowledge, new possibilities. Today's training, of course, falls in the category of new knowledge. Think about the person at your table who seemed most receptive to trying the buttermilk. Then, try to emulate his or her enthusiasm as you learn some things that contradict your attitudes or assumptions or experience. And, if no one at your table was willing to alter his or her usual behavior, think about the fact that most of us would not even be here today if we did not have pioneers of one sort or another in our family history!

5

FLUBS & DUBS

FORM

This activity is designed to reduce the tension that characterizes the first hour of training, when people do not know one another, are afraid to speak up, or may feel uncomfortable because someone beside them has a higher position in the company. In a sense, the activity establishes a common denominator among participants, assuring them that they are all equal, at least during the course of the training. They are all learners.

The activity works best with a group of 20 or fewer, because you will need at least one minute for each person to introduce himself or herself via "the worse mistake I ever made in my career." Begin by sharing the worst mistake you ever made in your own career, keeping the story succinct. Tell how it turned out, what you learned from it, and how it has shaped subsequent actions. Then call on each person to share—essential points only—the silliest thing, the most embarrassing scenario, or the worst mistake associated with their careers thus far.

Because some of these stories will be funny, others poignant, others eye-opening, this icebreaker works quickly to establish collegiality among participants.

FUNCTION

1. Before class begins, appoint one person as judge. He or she will award the participant who had the best worst-case scenario a token prize. (The most outstanding flubber could also be given a certificate made out in advance to recognize the "King of Flubs" or the "Queen of Errors" for his or her courage in sharing the flub story with the group.)

2. Begin by sharing your own worst-mistake-I-ever-made story and then call on participants to give their names and their own stories.

3. As they are speaking, quickly and unobtrusively list on the flip chart the essential lessons learned. (Note: If anyone is rambling, gently say, "Just a few more seconds, please, Bill.")

4. Ask the judge to crown the person who had the most unusual (or most funny, most horrible, most disastrous, etc.) flub.

FOLLOW-UP

Encourage participants to realize that mistakes are a normal and natural part of the learning process. One way they can do this is by reading about those who profit from mistakes—their own and others'. For example, in the July, 1995, issue of *USAir Magazine*, page 48, Bill Gates spoke of the importance of making mistakes. He asserted, "It's fine to celebrate success, but it is more important to heed the lessons of failure."

TRANSITION

You have before you living proof of the fact that there is life after corporate mistakes. Keep these stories on the back burner of your mind's stove as we proceed with the course. Don't let the fear of making a mistake prevent you from fully participating in the events I have planned for this workshop. Don't let worry about appearing foolish keep you from asking questions or making comments. Contribute as much as you can—that is the best way to add value to the training you will receive today.

6

I-OPENERS

FORM

This activity, which takes about 15 minutes, provides an excellent way for participants to get to know one another in a very short period of time. No materials, other than the worksheet, are necessary. Divide the class into triads and if one or two are left over, they can easily supplement other triads.

FUNCTION

1. Distribute the I-Opener worksheet. Ask participants to skim the entire sheet before starting to work.

2. After allowing a few seconds for them to scan the paper, tell them to select five statements and complete them. Once this is done, ask them to look over their answers and then to complete the statement at the bottom, "The most interesting thing about me is...."

3. Next, have participants share their answers with the other members of their triad. After listening to each member, the remaining two will answer the prompts at the bottom of the worksheet ("The most interesting thing I learned about the second person in my triad is..." and "The most interesting thing I learned about the third person in my triad is...").

4. Call on one person in each triad to introduce the other persons in the group to the whole class by simply saying, "I am _____ and the most interesting thing about me is _____. This is _____ and the most interesting thing about her is _____. The third person in our triad is _____ and the most interesting thing about him is _____."

FOLLOW-UP

Encourage participants to prepare their own list of prompts and to start their own team or staff meetings with a different prompt each week. Sample inclusions might be: "The best thing that happened to me this past week was..." or "The toughest problem I am grappling with is...."

TRANSITION

So often, we are so busy working that we don't take time to know the people with whom we are working. The same is true in a training program—we are so busy learning that we don't take time to know others, who could assist us in our learning, just as colleagues can assist us in our working.

Many of the assignments you will be given today will require team effort. Now that you know a little more about the people in this room, I hope you will feel more comfortable working with them. Don't forget what Don Petersen, former head of Ford Motor Company, had to say about productivity: "Results depend on relationships."

I-OPENERS WORKSHEET

Directions: Check off five statements and complete them in reference to the work you do. Then review your answers and decide what is most interesting about you. Write that thought at the end of this worksheet and do the same after listening to the other people in your triad.

❑   I've attained _____.

❑   I break _____.

❑   I concentrate on _____.

❑   I define _____.

❑   I establish _____.

❑   I finalize _____.

❑   I gather _____.

❑   I hunt for _____.

❑   I idolize _____.

❑   I juggle _____.

❑   I know _____.

❑   I've learned _____.

❑   I make _____.

❑   I nourish _____.

❑   I organize _____.

❑   I produce _____.

❑ I question _____.

❑ I've reengineered _____.

❑ I satisfy _____.

❑ I treat _____.

The most interesting thing about me is_____.

The most interesting thing about the second person in my triad is _____.

The most interesting thing about the third person in my triad is _____.

7

I'M NOT CONFUSED. I'M JUST WELL MIXED!

FORM

Participants will work in small groups on this exercise, which asks them to unscramble words (related to training) whose letters have been well mixed. The whole activity will take about 15 minutes. You may wish to award token prizes, such as copies of articles pertinent to the training topic, to the team that first figures out the answers to the handout problems.

FUNCTION

1. Introduce the exercise with this mini-lecture:

Defending himself against aspersions of addlepatedness, poet Robert Frost once asserted, "I'm not confused. I'm just well mixed." New knowledge can sometimes seem confusing, when in fact it is just well mixed. I have mixed together the elements I feel are most cogent for the training you will receive today. At first, I suspect, this new knowledge will appear confusing, for it will be different from what you have known, what you have done in the past.

I will need you to trust my ability to design curriculum and to convey the concepts in a logical fashion—even though it may not seem that way at all in the beginning. This exercise will illustrate how understanding can be achieved through perseverance and the willingness to demystify structural elements of a given word, in this case, or of a concept.

2. Have participants find a partner to work with. As they are doing this, distribute Handout 7-1.

3. Allow time to complete the task then check the answers of the winning pair:

1— <u>basketball</u>, paper, pencil, flip chart, marking pens

2— instructor, <u>lawnmower</u>, participants, guest lecturer, managers

3— concepts, ideas, discussion, questions, <u>eggplant</u>

4. Award the token prizes.

FOLLOW-UP

Using the worksheet as an example, this exercise could serve very well as a midpoint energizer or even as a closer. Ask table groups to list the ten words they found most relevant to the training topic. Then have them scramble the words and exchange them with another table group.

Ask for a group of volunteers to work with the editor of the organizational newsletter in sponsoring a monthly contest of scrambled words that relate to the field or industry in which participants work.

TRANSITION

I've chosen this exercise to illustrate an important cognitive concept, one that educator John Dewey probably expressed best when he noted, "The first step in learning is confusion." The scrambled words initially appeared foreign, unfamiliar, perhaps even unknowable. But you stuck with them, you brought clarity to the chaos by unscrambling the well-mixed letters.

Some of the material I will present to you today will be confusing at first. But I encourage you to do what you have done with these letters: Stick with it. Ask for clarification. Discuss the issues with your teammates. In time, these concepts will also become clear to you.

HANDOUT 7-I

Directions: Four of the five words in each set of problems below are related to each other and to training as well. However, there is one word in each set that has nothing to do with learning. Your task is to unscramble the words so you know what each one is and also what the unrelated word is. A simple example would be this, related to the realm of management:

NLPA, TRCDIE, RHEI, RJGAAU, ICDDEE.

The fourth word, "jaguar," does not fit with other managerial functions: "plan," "direct," "hire," and "decide."

1.   What word does not belong? _____
a)   AATSLLEKBB
b)   PPARE
c)   LIPCEN
d)   PLIF RTCHA
e)   GKNMRAI NSPE

2.   What word does not belong? _____
a)   IRRTTOUNSC
b)   RWWOENLMA
c)   STPPAAIIRCTN
d)   TEUSG RREECUTL
e)   GSRAAEMN

3.   What word does not belong? _____
a)   CCEOSTPN
b)   SAEID
c)   SSSIIOUNCD
d)   EIOTQUNSS
e)   GGNEPTAL

8

INITIAL INTERROGATIONS

FORM

Pre- and posttraining assessments are done by participants on their attitudes toward training. Participants take a few minutes to fill out the first worksheet and then use it as an introduction to share selected information with a partner. At the end of the training, participants receive the second worksheet and compare it to the first to learn more about their actual performance as compared to their predicted performance.

FUNCTION

1. As participants enter the training room, greet each one and hand him or her a copy of Handout 8-1. Invite them to take a seat anywhere and to complete the worksheets as soon as they are seated.

2. Begin the class with a brief introduction of yourself and the course objectives. (Encourage participants, if they have not already done so, to complete the worksheets as you are speaking.)

3. Mention they have had a chance to learn a little about you. Now, they will have a chance to learn more about their fellow learners. Have participants work with one or two others and, using the worksheet as a reference, introduce themselves to their partner(s). They should use only those worksheet questions they feel comfortable discussing.

FOLLOW-UP

Participants can use the same questions on the two worksheets each time they attend a training program. At the end of 6 months, they can reevaluate their attitudes and self-assessments.

They can also use similar questionnaires prior to and at the end of any number of work-related events, such as meetings, being introduced to a new supervisor, or joining a new team.

TRANSITION

Thank you for taking the time to engage in some introspection. I'd like you to hold on to these forms because at the end of our training session, I'm going to hand out a similar form, which I'll ask you to fill out then. You'll have an opportunity at that time to compare your estimates with reality.

Our objective today, of course, is to have you learn more than you already know about [Mention the course title]. In the process, though, you will learn more about others and certainly more about yourself. In fact, if you leave here at the end of the training program the same person you were when you walked in, then you and I will both have failed to meet our objectives.

HANDOUT 8-1

Directions: Answer each of the questions as honestly as you can by placing an *X* on the continuum to reflect the actions or attitudes you will probably demonstrate during the course of the training. Next, tell why you placed the *X* where you did. You will be asked to share a few of these assessments with a partner.

1.   How much do you plan to contribute? |_____|
                                                  Not at all   Fully

Why? _____

2.   How do you feel about being here? |_____|
                                                  I'd rather be at work   It's a growth opportunity

Why? _____

3.   How do you feel about learning in general? |_____|
                                                  I know all I need to know   I can never learn
                                                  to do my job   enough

Why? _____

4.   How much do you know about this topic? |_____|
                                                  Very little   Probably more than
                                                                                                the instructor

Why? _____

5.   How good a listener are you? |_____|
                                                  I haven't heard any complaints   I admit I'm a poor
                                                                                                    listener

Why? _____

6.   Will you apply what you've learned? |_____|
                                                  Probably not   My boss expects me to
                                                                                            use what I've learned

Why? _____

HANDOUT 8-2

Directions: Answer each of these questions as honestly as you can by placing an *X* on the continuum and then stating why you placed the *X* where you did. Then compare your answers to the ones on Handout 8-1.

1. How much did you contribute? |_____|
                                     Not at all   Fully

Why? _____

2. How do you feel about having been here? |_____|
                                     I'd rather have been at work   It's a growth opportunity

Why? _____

3. How do you feel about learning in general? |_____|
                                     I know all I need to know   I realize how
                                     to do my job   little I know

Why? _____

4. How much do you know about this topic? |_____|
                                     Not enough   More than I realized

Why? _____

5. How many notes did you take? |_____|
                                     None   Enough to share the
                                                                  content with others

Why? _____

6. Will you apply what you've learned? |_____|
                                     Probably not   Absolutely

Why? _____

9

LET ME INTRODUCE MYSELF

FORM

A bit of creativity is required for this opener. As participants introduce themselves to others in their table groups of five or six, they will add a plastic flower to a flower pot with each introduction and will then prepare a description of how their arrangement reflects their group assemblage. These descriptions will then be shared with the other groups. Altogether, the activity takes about 15 minutes.

Before the start of class, you will place a flower pot (filled with florists' foam) in the center of each table. You also need to gather enough plastic flowers so each group can have a wide selection from which to choose. (Note: You can obtain the flowers inexpensively by going to discount stores or garage sales in the weeks preceding the course.) Place the flowers in plastic bags, one bag for each table group.

FUNCTION

1. Arrange table groups of five or six participants each. Explain that they will have an opportunity to demonstrate their artistry as they introduce themselves to each other. Point out that each table group has a flower pot. Walk to each table group and deliver a bag of flowers, explaining that as each person introduces himself or herself, he or she will simultaneously be selecting a flower and adding it to the pot.

2. Once the introductions are complete, ask participants to jointly write no more than one written paragraph explaining how the arrangement resembles them as a group.

3. After a few minutes, ask a spokesperson from each group to read the paragraph.

4. An optional extension would be to ask an outsider to judge the flower arrangements. You could then award the winning team a set of marking pens.

FOLLOW-UP

At the end of the class, ask each person to write on a 3 x 1-inch strip of paper the most valuable thing he or she learned. Staple each person's statement to one of the flowers and give each participant a flower as a parting gift. Ask that they keep the flowers in their work stations as constant reminders of the new knowledge they have acquired and the need to continuously apply and add to it.

TRANSITION

Let these flowers symbolize the work we have ahead of us today. The company has provided the foundation, the framework, and the resources for you to be in attendance today. The flower pot symbolizes this. Each of you has something to add to the basic arrangement. The flowers represent your contributions. And while these plastic flowers cannot grow, real flowers can. But...they need nurturing. And that means, once the training is over, it will be up to you to help it continue to grow.

10

PRIORITY PARTNERS

FORM

This activity requires participants to select their top priority regarding training and then to find someone else in the room who has chosen the same priority. In total, the exercise requires about 10 minutes. It will very quickly provide you with insight into participants' priorities regarding what you are about to deliver. Regard the information you will receive as an opportunity to adapt your plans to the needs expressed by these "customers."

FUNCTION

1.   As participants enter the training room, greet them at the door and hand them a copy of Handout 10-1. Ask them to read it and make a selection.

2.   Once everyone has entered, ask them to stand and find another person in the room who has made the same selection. They are to introduce themselves to that person and then the pair will continue going around the room, finding all the others who have made that same selection. With each new inclusion to their groups, they will continue to make introductions. (Those who cannot find another or many other same-priority partners can form their own group and introduce themselves to each other even though they have different priorities.)

3.   Ask the newly formed groups to remain seated together at least until this next step is finished: Call upon one person from each group to explain the collective rationale behind their selection of the priority they chose. (If there was a group of nonpartners, ask them to share the selections they made individually.)

FOLLOW-UP

Suggest that participants discuss priorities with their supervisors when they return to the job. They can begin by asking the supervisor what was his or her top priority or primary objective for sending the participant to the training session.

They can then explain what their own top priorities were. If there is a mismatch, further discussion between participants and their supervisors should follow. If, in fact, the objectives are parallel, it will be easier for participants to use the knowledge they have acquired in the most appropriate way possible.

TRANSITION

Your organization has made an investment in you—an expensive investment. While you are here, of course, your work is not getting done. So, as necessary and critical as training is, we could say that we lose one whole day's worth of productivity while you are here. Clearly, the organization is willing to forego that productivity in order to provide you with knowledge you don't currently have.

Furthermore, they are willing to spend money on books and materials, printing and equipment, refreshments, and my salary as well. But they want something in return for this investment they are making in you. They want you to emerge more skilled at the end of the day than you were at the beginning. No matter what your top priority was, please remember for the rest of our training session that we have an obligation, each of us, to give something back. That something is not only a larger knowledge base but also the commitment to use our increased knowledge when we return to work.

HANDOUT 10-1

Directions: Listed below are reasons why employees attend training sessions. Place a check mark in front of the reason that reflects your personal top priority.

- ❏ To reinforce/review/refresh my "old" skills

- ❏ To learn how I can make my job easier

- ❏ To learn more about group dynamics

- ❏ To acquire new knowledge

- ❏ To satisfy my supervisor, who made me come here

- ❏ To flesh out my professional portfolio

- ❏ To obtain a certificate of completion/achievement

- ❏ To develop skills I will need in the future

- ❏ To acquire skills I can use as soon as I return to the job

- ❏ To have a chance to voice my opinion

- ❏ To escape from my supervisor/coworkers/job/customers for a day

- ❏ To have fun

- ❏ To convince my supervisor I am interested in continuous knowledge

- ❏ To make me more marketable

- ❏ To meet new people

Now, explain what you can do to help ensure your priority is met. _____

_____

_____

11

WHEN YOU ASK A DUMB QUESTION

FORM

As a tone-setter, this activity encourages participants to ask questions. Working in small groups of four or five, they will list at least five questions (on 3 x 5-inch cards) for you to answer. This opener takes about 15 minutes to conduct (or longer, if you choose to answer the questions in depth). Not only can participants tune in to the training that will follow because the questions hanging over their heads will have been answered, but you will also be able to get a feel for what concerns they may have, and to address those concerns, from the very start.

FUNCTION

1.   Present this mini-lecture at the very beginning of the session.

You've no doubt heard it said that the only stupid question is the one you did not ask. It's a slant on training with which I agree. In fact, a mind much greater than my own expressed the same sentiment thousands of year ago. Aristotle pointed out, "When you ask a dumb question, you get a smart answer."

Today, I'd like you and your team members to ask at least five questions you feel should be answered by me before we officially get under way with our training. Discuss those questions among you and then select five to write on these 3 x 5-inch cards.

2.   Distribute the cards.

3.   After about 10 minutes, collect the cards, shuffle them, and begin addressing them.

FOLLOW-UP

No doubt, there are questions employees have about particular elements of their jobs—what work is done, why it is done in the way it is done, why other things are not being done, et cetera. Encourage the formation of a group that will collect employee questions on a monthly basis for submission to management. If possible, serve as the liaison between the question askers and the question answerers.

TRANSITION

You must realize by now that I welcome questions. To me, they indicate you are actively contemplating this material rather than passively ingesting it. For the remainder of the session, please ask me relevant questions about the concepts I am presenting and the skills you are developing. I only ask that you wait for the appropriate time—the question you are just about to ask may be the one I am just about to answer. As you listen to the lecture or as you watch the video, for example, jot down whatever questions you may have. Then, if they are not answered by the end of the lecture or video, ask away!

12

SQUARE: WON

FORM

Participants will have a chance to fill in the quadrants of a square (shown on a transparency) in relation to the anticipated benefits they are seeking. They will use the squares they draw to introduce themselves to three other participants. As a group of four, participants will then present a summary of their square comments. This opener will take about 20 minutes to complete.

FUNCTION

1. Ask a series of questions to introduce this opener and hold a brief discussion based on these questions:

When was the last time you had "that winning feeling"?

What exactly causes us to feel like winners?

What are the circumstances surrounding winning, in the most general sense of the word?

2. Continue with this mini-lecture:

As a trainer, I work hard to ensure that you will leave the training sessions feeling like intellectual winners. To help me in creating that feeling, I need to know what constitutes training success as far as you are concerned. I'd like each of you right now to draw a large square on your papers and then to divide it into four quadrants. These represent the four main categories that are typically associated with successful learning. Now, label the quadrants as shown on this transparency.

3. Show Transparency 12-1 now and allow about 5 minutes for participants to complete it. You may wish to further explain each quadrant by asking, for example:

For the Knowledge quadrant, what do you want to learn? What skills do you hope to acquire? What do you expect to know when you leave this training?

In terms of Challenges, what would constitute success for you? What would make you feel like a winner? How far do you want to be stretched?

Many believe that if there is no behavioral change accompanying new knowledge, then there is no point in acquiring that knowledge. What do you expect to do differently as a result of this training?

When the training session is over, how do you want to feel? (Be specific.)

4. Divide the class into teams of four. Ask them to share their comments.

5. After 5 minutes or so, ask them to begin working on a group synthesis, which will be shared with the whole class.

6. Call on a spokesperson from each team to share the summary.

FOLLOW-UP

If you record the main points of each summary on flip chart paper and keep it posted during the training session, you can refer to these winning elements later when you bring closure to the training session.

Suggest that participants do a similar square for their jobs, their careers, their lives. To drift through life without periodically doing a reality check—prompted by these definitions of success, for example—is to live without goals. Such a lifestyle seldom results in the feeling that we have won the game of business or of life.

TRANSITION

Now that I have a better sense of what you want from this class, I can incorporate those expectations into the curriculum I have planned for you. Let's begin right now with challenges. The lecture I'm about to present to you now will indeed be a challenge....

WHAT I WANT FROM THIS CLASS:

Feelings	Knowledge
Changes	Challenges

13

THE CUBE OF INTELLECT

FORM:

Working in small groups of six or seven on this opener, participants ideally will realize the value of teamwork in both the instructional and the workplace setting. (If the realization does not evolve from the brainteaser activity, you can make mention of it anyway.) Altogether, the activity, shown on Transparency 13-1, takes about 15 minutes.

FUNCTION

1.   Begin by showing the transparency. Allow as much time as the teams need to figure out the correct answer: 144.

2.   Ask the first team that figured out the correct answer how they came up with it. (One can visualize slicing the rows of cubes and counting them separately or one can use the mathematical principle that says the volume of a solid object equals length times width times height [6 x 4 x 6].)

3.   Point out that within any given team or class or workplace site are people with varying skills. Some can visualize well, others excel at spatial relationships, others are math whizzes. When talents are combined, work is not only done more efficiently, it is done with more ease and greater quality.

4.   Relate these points to the theory of intelligence espoused by J.P. Guilford, who asserts that intelligence (typically measured by math and verbal scores alone) is actually a cube, with more than 100 separate and distinct types of knowledge.

FOLLOW-UP

Lead a discussion of the types of intelligence that may not be prized in our school systems but that represent intelligence nonetheless. Guilford, for example, found that there is musical intelligence, athletic intelligence, leadership intelligence, etc.

Ask participants to list all the kinds of intelligence they themselves possess (at least ten items should appear on their lists). Then ask them to star those with which they can make a contribution to this training session. Next ask them to check those that could lend value to the work they do. Using the same list, have them place a circle in front of those their supervisors know they possess. Finally, ask them to place an X beside those being used in the work they do.

Having identified the gaps between what they can offer and what is being tapped, participants and their supervisors can better optimize the extant talent within the organization.

TRANSITION

There are many approaches to settling the issues we will identify today. Numerous techniques can help us solve problems and resolve concerns—whether we are dealing with them in the classroom or at the work site. To believe that any one person has all the answers all the time is to doom ourselves to mediocrity. I'd like you to use your own potential, of course, to the fullest extent possible as we work together today. But I'd also like you to realize the person beside you has just as much potential. Please ensure that everyone's ideas are listened to as we proceed through this course.

How many small cubes within the large cube?

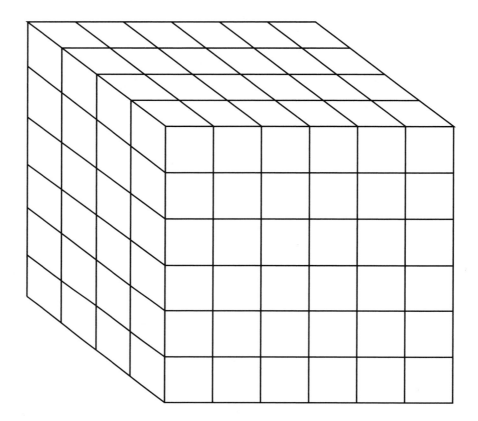

14

LIFE LINES

FORM

This opener helps participants get a sense of the big picture and their place within it. First, they work on their individual life lines and share them with two or three others. Then, two groups will join to develop an organizational life line. Finally, larger groups will merge to create an industry life line that projects 10 years into the future. The activity requires at least 15 minutes for completion.

FUNCTION

1.   Begin by drawing your own life line on the flip chart. (The sample shown has been divided into 10-year increments.)

2.   Ask participants to draw life lines of their own, with more detail than shown in the example.

3.   Have them join one or two others and share their graphics.

4.   Next, ask each small group to join one other and to draw an organizational life line. (Note: If participants represent several different organizations, each person can do one for his or her own firm and they can then share the results.)

5.   The groups (numbering four to six participants by now) will merge with one other group to draw an industry life line. (Note: Should they come from a wide variety of industries, they can do a life line for the country instead, indicating the most significant events in the last 400 years and projecting 100 years ahead.)

6.   Toss out this question: "How might the training you are about to receive impact the future events you have projected onto your life lines, organizational life lines, or industry life lines?" Lead a discussion focusing on the ability of knowledge to shape the future.

FOLLOW-UP   Suggest that participants prepare a professional life line, divided into 2-year increments, and that they make copies to share with a few close friends or colleagues. The friends should follow through periodically to see if the articulated goals have been met, if they should be adjusted, or if new ones should be set.

TRANSITION   *The training you will receive today is designed not only to enhance your own future but, ideally, to increase the likelihood that you will make an even more valuable contribution to the organization's future. To be sure, that future will look very little like the past—although, clearly, certain core values will always be at the foundation. What you will learn today will better prepare you to meet your own goals for the future and also increase your ability to help the organization meet its goals...one of which is to develop the knowledge base of all employees.*

15

MATCHING WITS

FORM

There are two purposes underlying this opener: (1) to develop awareness of the need to shift paradigms or reconfigure knowledge, to look at situations from a perspective other than the usual; and (2) to symbolize the power of desire linked to training. This short exercise can be completed in about 5 minutes.

FUNCTION

1. Preface the showing of Transparency 15-1 by noting that you need to get the group's cerebral juices flowing, as the information you are going to share with them today will be challenging and substantial.

2. Divide the group into dyads or triads.

3. Show the transparency and allow about 5 minutes for the groups to figure out the answer.

4. If no one is able to rearrange the matchsticks to spell:

Announce the answer.

5. Conclude with this brief tie-up:

When we are open to taking what we have, what we know, and reconfiguring it, we are often able to create valuable changes to existing practices. In fact, "vision" has been described by Jonathan Swift as "the art of seeing the invisible." Throughout this training session, I will be asking you to keep an open mind, to look at the old in a new way, to shift your ideas, to combine elements that perhaps you would never have thought of combining before. I suspect you'll find that some of these new concepts will be akin to T.N.T. in their impact on organizational thinking.

Collect and share other matchstick tricks, such as these.
(1) Rearrange the matches so these two triangles become four.

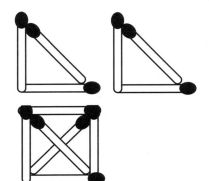

Answer:

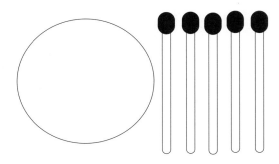

(2) Use these five matchsticks to create fourteen pieces in this circle.

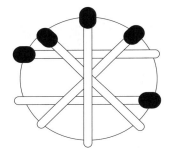

Answer:

Now that you have had a chance to match wits with one another, let's take a look at what we'll be doing from this point until the first break. I hope the same spirit of cooperation and friendly competition that existed while you worked on the puzzle continues all day long.

Move only three matches to form a powerful, acronymic word.

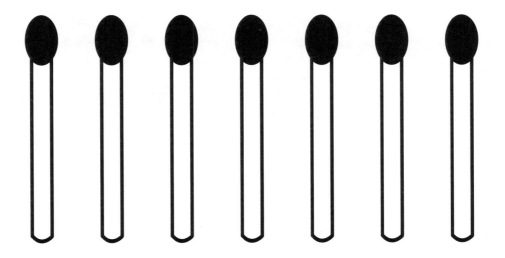

16

PAST, PRESENT, & FUTURE

FORM

With just a few moments' worth of introspection, participants will know a bit more about themselves and, at the same time, will have a vehicle to use as they introduce themselves to other persons in their small groups (five or six is an ideal number). This opener takes about 10 minutes. The only preparation for it is the duplication of Handout 16-1.

FUNCTION

1.   Pass out copies of Handout 16-1 and give participants 2–3 minutes to complete it. Advise them to be as serious or as funny, as officious or as offbeat as they wish when they work on it.

2.   Then ask them to join a small group and to select one item from the worksheet they would like to use in order to introduce themselves to the group.

3.   Afterwards, call on one spokesperson from each group and ask if there were any unusual findings; for example, did most members of the group turn out to be explorers?

FOLLOW-UP

Ask each person to draw three circles on the back of the worksheet and to label them Present, Past, and Future. Then play amateur psychologist as you interpret the circles:

Whichever circle is largest is the area in which the person is living his or her life. Conversely, the smallest circle reflects the least amount of concentration. Just as there are people who have managed to put the past behind them, there are those who cannot. (Their past circles appear large.) Just as there are those who are constantly tuned to the future (e.g., they have saved substantially for the rainy days), there are those who have made no provisions at all.

If the circles intersect, the individual has achieved a good balance among present, past, and future.

If the circles are concentric (with the present the largest of the three circles and the past the smallest), the person has learned how to live for the moment without neglecting the preparations necessary for the future.

Ask participants to discuss in their table groups how each word might apply to their post-training lives. For example, to what action plan can they *commit*? How might others *resist* participants' efforts to effect change as a result of the training they have received?

TRANSITION

Working adults often value training not only for what they learn about the subject at hand, but for what they learn about themselves as well. Most of us are so busy doing more with less that we simply don't have time to think about the direction in which we are heading. Exercises like this one help us get a handle on our intentions.

Keep the worksheet in front of you throughout the day. Whenever you hear or see something that relates to one of the words on it, make a note or two. For example, if I should mention a book you think is worth reading, write down its title and author beside the word "explore."

HANDOUT 16-1

Directions: The line below is a continuum divided into three sections: Past, Present and Future. Beneath the line are other lines with two opposing words at each end. In the few minutes' time allotted, fill in as many examples as you can in relation to the presented word and time. For example, if the words were "deny" and "commit," perhaps you *denied* problems existed in the past, but in the present, you are *committed* to solving those problems. If you have not yet made a commitment but will in the future, you would describe that commitment in the Future column.

PAST	PRESENT	FUTURE
Resist		Explore
Find		Seek
Lost		Found
Control		Yield
Accept		Avoid
Pretend		Acknowledge
Fear		Welcome
Withhold		Give

17

CALLING CARDS

FORM

Interaction is called for with this opener, which requires participants to fill in the blanks on a handout (anonymously). The handouts are then shuffled and each person receives someone else's. The time required will vary, depending on the size of the group, but you can plan on approximately 1 minute per person plus 2–3 minutes for the worksheet to be filled in.

FUNCTION

1. Distribute copies of Handout 17-1 and ask participants to complete as many of the items as they can within the allotted time.

2. Collect the worksheets and shuffle them.

3. Give each person one worksheet (other than his or her own).

4. Call on one person to start. He or she will select one item from the handout, stand, and announce, "I'd like to meet the person who wrote _____ [reading from the handout]." The person will then sit down.

5. The person who wrote the statement will stand and give his or her name and a brief elaboration of the statement. Then this person will make the same announcement, selecting one item from the handout he or she is holding.

6. Continue until every person has been introduced.

FOLLOW-UP

Recommend that participants use these handouts in the following way upon their return to work. They should make a copy (minus their answers) and give it to their supervisors to fill out (in relation to the employee). Then, the employee and his or her supervisor sit down and share their answers and outlooks.

TRANSITION

Now that each of us knows a little more about the other travelers on this learning journey we have embarked upon, let me tell you a little more about the course itself and my objectives for it.

HANDOUT 17-1

Directions: Look over the following prompts. Select at least three and complete the statements in relation to your work experience. Do not put your names on this paper.

✪   The thing that most prevents me from doing the very best work of which I am capable is

_____

✪   The thing I do best in relation to my job is _____

✪   I wish I had an opportunity to _____

✪   One thing that would improve our productivity, in my opinion, is _____

✪   The biggest barrier to efficiency in my workplace is _____

✪   I believe leaders should _____

✪   Our customers, I believe, most want _____

✪   The most important element in teamwork is _____

✪   The most valued aspect of a manager's work, I feel, is _____

✪   The biggest time waster in my workplace is _____

✪   Stress in our organization is primarily caused by _____

✪   I think this training _____

✪   My career path _____

✪   I would define *quality* as _____

✪   Trust in our organization is _____

✪   Power in our organization is _____

✪   The way decisions are made where I work is _____

✪   When I solve problems, I _____

✪   One way to increase motivation among employees is _____

✪   As far as communications are concerned, my department _____

18

DON'T HAVE/DON'T WANT

FORM

Determining individual learning needs is the purpose behind this opener, which takes 5–10 minutes to execute. Participants fill out a square, using the transparency as a model, and then share their insights with one or two others.

FUNCTION

1.   Explain that just as you have objectives for the training to be presented, most participants enter the training room with objectives of their own. Typically, these are not written down. Sometimes, they are only half-articulated. But, you'd like to have them spend a few minutes ascertaining their own training needs.

2.   Show Transparency 18-1. Give these examples for each quadrant:

The upper left-hand quadrant asks you to think about those things you currently want and currently have—at least as far as training is concerned. An example might be a positive attitude toward learning.

Next to that is the box calling for things you currently have but don't want—for example, an impatience that prevents you from going in-depth with your knowledge acquisition. In the box beneath that, please record those things you don't have and don't want, in other words, what you should avoid. One for-instance could be a feeling of superiority about what you know. Or, it could be a promotion, meaning you are here for the sake of learning and not for the sake of your career.

Finally, please consider those things you want but don't yet have, such as expertise in this area we are learning more about today.

3.   After a few minutes, have participants work with one or two others and share their observations.

4.   Ask each dyad or triad to select one item from one quadrant they found most interesting. Have a spokesperson from each small group share that response.

FOLLOW-UP   Encourage participants to engage in a similar assessment as far as their job responsibilities are concerned. To illustrate, in the have/don't want category could lie possibilities for streamlining the work by possibly eliminating some aspects of it or at least reducing the amount of time required for less-favored tasks.

TRANSITION   *Now that you have had a chance to think about what you would like from this training, let me share what I would like. These are the instructional goals for the class [Enumerate them]. And this is an overview of the course content [Share it now]. Additionally, I'd like each of you to relax, enjoy the learning journey, and participate in it as fully as you can.*

	Want	**Don't want**
Have		
Don't have		

19

THE DAVE CLARK FIVE IS TAKING OVER

FORM

Participants will enjoy hearing predictions that never materialized. They will then be asked to think of some from their own lives (personal or professional) and to share those with others in groups of four or five. Allow about 10 minutes for this opener.

FUNCTION

1. Share the following information with the class:

More than 30 years ago, a music critic for a Baltimore newspaper predicted the Beatles would lose their popularity and that the Dave Clark Five would replace them in the hearts of music lovers.

Other predictions that have proven unreliable over the years include:

Lord Kelvin: "X-rays are a hoax."

Richard van der Riet Wooley (royal astronomer): "Space travel is utter bilge."

Physicist Lee DeForest: "I have not the smallest molecule of faith in aerial navigation other than ballooning."

Clark Woodward: "As far as sinking a ship with a bomb is concerned, it just can't be done."

Octave Chanute: "The [flying] machines will eventually be fast; they will be used in sport but they should not be thought of as commercial carriers."

2. Share with the group a prediction that was made about you or your abilities. An example follows:

When I was in fourth grade, Mrs. Hogeboom called on me to write something on the blackboard. When I finished, she stood there for a moment staring at my handwriting, and then pronounced, "You, my dear, have schoolteacher's handwriting." Bam! My fate was sealed. One simple utterance from Mrs. Hogeboom and my future was decided. I stand before you today as living proof of her prediction of what I was to become.

3.   Now ask participants to think about predictions that were made about them early in their lives or careers and how accurate those predictions turned out to be. (If participants prefer, they can recall predictions that were made about their organization, their managers, their product or service, their industry, or about technology or changes that would affect the business community, such as the paperless office.)

4.   Form small groups of four or five and have participants share their insights with one another.

FOLLOW-UP

Encourage participants upon their return to work to discuss with industry experts, acknowledged authorities, or their own managers the trends in their field. They should then use the knowledge they have gleaned to think about changes that will probably occur and what they can do to prepare for them.

TRANSITION

Samuel Goldwyn may have been correct when he advised others to "never make predictions—especially about the future." Notwithstanding his advice, I'm going to make a prediction today: I predict you will learn more than you now know about [Mention name of training program]. *In fact, let me share with you the curricular outline of what's in store* [Review course outline now].

20

MEMORIES ARE MADE OF THIS

FORM

This opener is designed to provide you with information regarding what constitutes training excellence, in the opinion of participants. Additionally, it is designed to focus their thinking on those standards that represent high-quality training. (Incorporate as many as possible into the content and context of the training session you are conducting.) This opener will take about 15 minutes to conduct and needs no advance preparation other than making copies of the worksheet. Participants will work in teams of four or five.

FUNCTION

1.   Begin with a personal anecdote to illustrate your own recollection of memorable courses or instructors. (A sample follows.)

When I was in graduate school, I studied what I was drawn to. History was not one of the draws—never has been for me and probably never will be. However, we had a guest lecturer, for some reason, in our Cognitive Processes course one day, Professor Salamone. He spoke about Pericles, the great Greek statesman and general who lived 500 years before the birth of Christ. As Professor Salamone described Pericles on the Athens battlefields, history suddenly came alive for me—it has never happened before or since. I remember thinking, "Thank goodness I've never encountered such an instructor before. If I had, I would surely have majored in history and not education and human development."

To establish a learning-receptive atmosphere here today, I'm going to ask you to think about memorable moments from training you have had in the past.

2.   Distribute Handout 20-1 and ask participants to complete it and then to join three or four others.

3.   Team members will introduce themselves using the worksheet and will then work to prepare a synthesis, specifying the components of excellent learning conditions.

4.   Ask a spokesperson from each team to share the syntheses.

5.   As they do so, record the main points on the flip chart and refer to them periodically as the training proceeds.

FOLLOW-UP   Recommend that employees engage in a similar exercise related to ideal working conditions. Then, they can form teams committed to creating those very conditions.

TRANSITION   *Thank you for this input. For my part, I will attempt to replicate as many of these positive elements as I can in order to make this training session a memorable one. One way, of course, is not only to bring clarity to the information I will be sharing but also to clarify the expectations for the course.* [Highlight this or a comparable item on the flip chart list.] *Here's what will be expected of you during the next two days* [Substitute exact length of the training].

HANDOUT 20-1

Directions: Take a moment to recollect some of the instructional situations you felt were most conducive to learning. Go as far back as you like—it's not only college professors or corporate trainers who have effective teaching techniques! Once you have a few of these situations in mind, answer the following questions.

1. What instructor stands out as being especially effective? Why?_____

_____

2. What subject or course did you most enjoy? Why?_____

_____

3. What course materials stand out in your mind? Why?_____

_____

4. What training or classroom stands out? Why?_____

_____

5. Which fellow students do you recall as having added to the learning environment? How?

_____

_____

6. What format has helped you absorb new knowledge most easily?_____

_____

7. How was knowledge from an ideal learning situation reinforced?_____

_____

8. Think of the worst instructor you have ever had. What made him or her ineffective?

_____

_____

9. What conditions are ideal learning conditions for you?_____

_____

10. What are you hoping will be part of today's training session?_____

_____

21

ANSWER ME THIS

FORM

Participants tackle three of ten challenging questions for this opener and then use their answers as introductory remarks to interact with other participants. Triads join other triads and each six-person team then votes on one answer to present to the group at large. The activity takes about 20 minutes. The only advance preparation required is to copy the handout.

FUNCTION

1. Point out that question asking and question answering are integral aspects of effective learning. (They are important aspects of leadership as well, according to Peter Drucker, who asserts "...exceptional leaders know how to ask questions—the right questions.")

2. Explain that you are about to distribute a worksheet of questions, which participants will then use to introduce themselves to two other people.

3. Once the triads' introductions are complete, each triad will join one other triad. The six-person teams will then each select one answer to present to the group at large.

4. Have one person in each team read the team's selection.

FOLLOW-UP

Depending on their circumstances, participants should begin collecting questions for future use. If their company is going through a downsizing cycle, for example, it would behoove participants to collect sample interview questions. If they will soon have a performance review, they should have questions ready to ask their supervisor. If they are engaged in a benchmarking project or have assembled a focus group, their success will depend on asking appropriate questions.

TRANSITION

It's been said that if you wish to receive, all you have to do is ask. What are some things you want to receive before this training program has ended? Ask me for them now and I'll do my best to give you the answers. For example,

Is anyone wondering when we will take breaks? [Answer these questions]

Does anyone want to know where the phones and rest rooms are?

Who is interested in learning when we will break for lunch?

Is someone eager to learn about the course objectives?

Who is wondering how this training relates to the work you do?

What other questions do you have for me?

HANDOUT 21-1

Directions: Briefly but specifically answer as many of the following questions as you can within the next 5 minutes. Then, you will use some or all of your answers to introduce yourself to two other participants.

1. Sam Walton encouraged his employees to "eliminate the dumb." What dumb practices in your workplace would you like to eliminate?_____

_____

2. If you were CEO of your organization, what is the first thing you would change?

_____

_____

3. What are some questions you can't answer?_____

_____

4. What motivates you to do your very best work?_____

_____

5. If your workplace were a sporting event, which one would it be and why?

_____

_____

6. What causes stress in your workplace?_____

_____

7. How do you intend to use this training when you return to work?_____

_____

8. What question(s) do you wish your boss would ask you?_____

_____

_____

9. How can creativity be fostered in your workplace?_____

_____

22

SEEING RED, WHITE, & BLUE

FORM

The elements of this opener (fifteen altogether) will be posted around the training room. If possible, have a patriotic token prize (or something else colored red, white, and blue) to award to the first team completing the exercise. In advance of the class, buy enough red, white, and blue adhesive circles (about an inch in diameter) for each participant to have five. Also, print the puzzles, one each on 15 sheets of 8½ X 11-inch white paper, and post them around the room.

FUNCTION

1. As participants enter the room, give each five red or white or blue adhesive circles. Also hand each participant a Directions strip (copy and cut Handout 22-1). (Note: Do not hand out the materials until at least six participants have arrived.)

2. Start the class 5 minutes past the official starting time, allowing participants the opportunity to complete the assignment, which requires each team of three to place one of its fifteen red, white, and blue circles on each of the 15 sheets of paper you have posted around the room if they know the solution to the puzzle. The sheets will have the following puzzles, one written on each of the 15 sheets with either red or blue marking pens. (Note: Only the capital letters should be written, of course, not the answers that appear in parentheses. Also, other correct answers are possible. For example, BV is listed here for the song "Blue Velvet," but some individuals may be more familiar with the product Black Velvet.)

DIMMBEB ("Don't It Make My Brown Eyes Blue?")
RS (Red Square)
WES (White Elephant Sale)
HFRO (*Hunt for Red October*)
JWS (January White Sale)
BSS ("Blue Suede Shoes")
BBM (Blue Bonnet Margarine)
WWR (White Water Rafting)
BAB (Black and Blue)
ITR (In the Red)
BV ("Blue Velvet")

WCOD (White Cliffs of Dover)
WL (White Lie)
OIABM (Once in a Blue Moon)
RRFABL ("Red Roses for a Blue Lady")
RAR, VAB ("Roses Are Red, Violets Are Blue")

3.   Start the session no more than 5 minutes after the official starting time by asking, "Did any team manage to get rid of all fifteen adhesive circles?" If so, they are the winning team. If not, ask, "Does any team have only one circle left?" Continue asking this question, increasing the leftover number by one each time, until you find the team with the fewest number of circles left. Ask them to quickly give the answers.

FOLLOW-UP   Depending on the nature of the training you are presenting, you can do a similar activity using phrases or titles associated with the topic. In a management class, for example, the abbreviation MBWA stands for "management by walking around." In a Quality Management course, DOF stands for Dr. Deming's exhortation to "drive out fear."

TRANSITION   *Now that you've had a chance to flex your mental muscles and to meet some colleagues in the process, we can get under way with our training. I hope nothing I say or do today will "make you see red." However, if you wish to offer a dissenting opinion, know that I welcome all points of view. On the other hand, if you are getting "blue" because you think I might call on you and you don't wish to answer, just shake your head and I'll move on to someone else.*

Directions: You have five adhesive circles, either red or white or blue. Please write your initials on your circles right now. In order to successfully complete this assignment, you must find two other people who have the colors you do *not* have. Your team of three, then, will have five red, five white, and five blue circles. As soon as you figure out one of the puzzles posted around the room, put an initialed circle on it. If you and your two partners are the first to get rid of all your circles (by placing one on each puzzle you've solved), you will be declared the official winners.

Directions: You have five adhesive circles, either red or white or blue. Please write your initials on your circles right now. In order to successfully complete this assignment, you must find two other people who have the colors you do *not* have. Your team of three, then, will have five red, five white, and five blue circles. As soon as you figure out one of the puzzles posted around the room, put an initialed circle on it. If you and your two partners are the first to get rid of all your circles (by placing one on each puzzle you've solved), you will be declared the official winners.

Directions: You have five adhesive circles, either red or white or blue. Please write your initials on your circles right now. In order to successfully complete this assignment, you must find two other people who have the colors you do *not* have. Your team of three, then, will have five red, five white, and five blue circles. As soon as you figure out one of the puzzles posted around the room, put an initialed circle on it. If you and your two partners are the first to get rid of all your circles (by placing one on each puzzle you've solved), you will be declared the official winners.

23

BIZ BUZ

FORM

Small groups will work together on Handout 23-1, which asks them to figure out common words associated with the business world. The words, though, are written phonetically. This opener takes only 5 minutes, but gives participants a chance to establish rapport within the first few minutes of class with at least a small group of colearners. Duplicate the handout prior to the start of class. If you wish, purchase token prizes for the winning team.

FUNCTION

1. Divide the group into teams of four or five.
2. Distribute Handout 23-1 and allow a few minutes for completion.
3. Award prizes for the team that finishes first with these answers:

        1—authority
        2—cultural diversity
        3—audit
        4—entrepreneur
        5—quality
        6—negotiation
        7—cooperation
        8—creativity
        9—empowerment
      10—customer
      11—decisions
      12—analysis
      13—imagination

4. Ask each team to select one word from the list and tell how the training they are about to receive relates to that word.

FOLLOW-UP

The same exercise can be adapted to phrases germane to the training topic being conducted and used at various points throughout the day.

TRANSITION

I certainly hope that the same enthusiasm and cooperative efforts I've seen with this exercise will be evidenced throughout our training day. Like these phonetically spelled words, the knowledge points I'll be making may initially seem disguised, may at first be unidentifiable because of their newness. But in time, understanding will be yours as we work with the various concepts and as you develop familiarity with them.

HANDOUT 23-1

Directions: As a team, figure out the word or phrase that is phonetically spelled and rewrite it in the blank space with the correct spelling. For example, "biz'nis" is really "business."

1. _____ əthor'ətē

2. _____ kul'chərəl dəvʉr' sətē

3. _____ ô' dit

4. _____ an' trəprənur'

5. _____ kwäl'ətē

6. _____ ni gō'shēa' shən

7. _____ kō äp'ər ā' shən

8. _____ kre' ā tiv'ətē

9. _____ im pȯu'ər mənt

10. _____ kus'təmər

11. _____ di sizh'ənz

12. _____ ənal'əsis

13. _____ i maj'ənā'shən

24

EX LIBRIS

FORM

Not only will participants have an opportunity to get to know one another via this opener, they will also be given an excellent reading list of possibilities. The exercise, which small groups of four or five will work on, takes about 5 minutes. If a discussion is held following the exercise, plan on another 10 minutes or so.

FUNCTION

1. Divide the class into teams of four or five.

2. Distribute Handout 24-1.

3. As soon as one team has finished, ask them to read their answers, which are: Tom Peters (*The Pursuit of WOW!*), Max DePree (*Leadership Is an Art*), Gillian Butler (*Managing Your Mind, with Tony Hope*), Michael LeBoeuf (*The World's Greatest Management Principle*), Jack Trout (*The New Positioning*), Rosabeth Moss Kanter (*World Class*), John Naisbitt (*Megatrends 2000*), Jack Stack (*The Great Game of Business*), Deborah Tannen (*Talking from 9 to 5*), Charles Handy (*Gods of Management*), Marsha Lewin (*The Overnight Consultant*), Patricia Aburdene (*Megatrends 2000*).

4. Ask if anyone has read any of these or other books by any of these authors. If so, ask that person to give a brief synopsis of the book(s) he or she has read. If no one has read any of the books, offer your own synopsis for one of the books you have recently read yourself.

FOLLOW-UP

Encourage participants to read the books listed on the handout. All appear in the Bibliography.

Have several of the books available. Periodically, hand one of the books to one of the participants. Give him or her 5 minutes to skim the book and then to share with the group at large one idea he or she especially likes.

TRANSITION

Many of the authors we've mentioned in this exercise are proposing some fairly radical concepts. Tom Peters, for example, insists that "if you have gone a whole week without being disobedient, you are doing yourself and your organization a disservice." I only ask that you give full consideration to the ideas you will hear today. Think about them, discuss them, poke and prod and probe them before deciding whether or not you can accept them. Do not be afraid to relinquish some of the deeply entrenched ideas you may have held thus far. A foolish consistency, as they say, is the hobgoblin of little minds.

Directions: In the column on the left are the first names of popular business authors. On the right side are the last names. Unfortunately, the names are all mixed up. Work with your team to determine which names go with which.

Tom	LeBoeuf
Max	Moss Kanter
Gillian	Handy
Michael	Trout
Jack	Lewin
Rosabeth	Peters
John	Aburdene
Jack	Naisbitt
Deborah	DePree
Charles	Butler
Marsha	Stack
Patricia	Tannen

25

SMARTS À LA WILL ROGERS

FORM

Groups of five or six compile their collective knowledge about the training topic via this opener, which takes about 10 minutes for the compilation and another 5–10 minutes for the reporting. The reports will allow you to quickly assess the extent of knowledge and sophistication about the training being presented. No equipment or material is required, other than paper and pencils (or flip chart and marking pens) for the teams to make their lists.

FUNCTION

1. Mention humorist Will Rogers' observation that we are all smart—it's just that we're smart about different things.

2. Divide participants into teams of five or six.

3. Ask each person to introduce himself or herself and then to list as many specific points as possible about the training topic. A team recorder captures the essential points from each person, eliminating repeated items.

4. Once each team member has given input, ask the teams to determine if they are Hungry for Knowledge (i.e., collectively, they know very little about the topic); Light on Learning (i.e., they already have a solid knowledge base); or Sated Scholars (i.e., as a group, they are ready for the advanced course).

FOLLOW-UP

At the conclusion of the training program, assemble the same teams and ask them to prepare a list (give them twice as much time as was allotted for the opening exercise) of what they know now. Ideally, the second lists will be at least twice as long as the first ones.

Collect articles on the topic so that participants who may have already grasped the basic concepts can be challenged by related views on the topic.

TRANSITION

I appreciate learning that some of you have done considerable study in this field. Given your backgrounds, experience, and expertise, I hope you will contribute as much as you can as our course progresses. I also appreciate knowing that some of you are virtual neophytes on this subject. Whenever possible, pair up with someone who has studied the subject quite a bit.

As you will understand, I hope, when the range of knowledge is as broad as we have here, it will be necessary for me to teach down the middle. If I am covering material you already know inside out, please just let me know. I have numerous other writings here that will provide you with challenging food for your mental appetites. On the other hand, if I am assuming an understanding you have not yet acquired, I will be happy to slow down and make my point more clearly. Just let me know. The first concept I'd like to present today is....

26

THE CHOICE IS YOURS

FORM

With this opener, participants will have a chance to establish rapport immediately with at least two others. They begin by completing the forced-choices worksheet themselves and then sharing their responses with two or three other participants. Altogether, the exercise takes 10–15 minutes.

FUNCTION

1. Distribute Handout 26-1. Allow about 5 minutes for completion.

2. Ask participants to join two or three others, then to introduce themselves and share their responses.

3. Ask each team to select one of the choices they feel best represents them as a group.

4. Have a spokesperson from each team introduce the members of the team and then explain why their selection reflects their collective essence.

FOLLOW-UP

Depending on the nature of the material being presented, additional worksheets could be prepared with items germane to the course material specifically rather than the general topic of training.

Handout 26-2, using antonyms at the end of continuum lines, is an example of a variation on the forced-choices theme. Although this handout deals with communications, it can easily be modified depending on the nature of the course. Given the fact, however, that communication pervades every aspect of our work and personal lives, the worksheet in itself makes an excellent opener by virtue of its "discussability."

TRANSITION

Now that you've had an opportunity to explore choices you have made in the past and choices you are likely to make in the future—at least as far as training is concerned—let me tell you about further choices you will be making today. Some of them are minor. You can choose, for example, to work alone, with a partner, or with a group for most of our training activities. You can choose to take notes or not take notes. Other choices are more significant. To illustrate, you can choose to apply the training after the session is over or you can choose to shelve it.

Of course, I hope you will make extensive use of the knowledge you have gained. I hope you choose to use that knowledge to increase your personal effectiveness and to make an even greater contribution to the organization that has arranged for you to have this training in the first place. The choice is yours!

HANDOUT 26-1

Directions: There are descriptors at the ends of each continuum line. The descriptors refer (in the loosest, most creative way possible) to ways that you might describe yourself as a learner and to the conditions under which your learning typically occurs. Don't spend much time analyzing the choices—you cannot make a wrong choice. Simply encircle the one that appeals to you. Once done, you will be asked to share your choices (and the rationale behind them) with two or three other participants.

1.   I prefer an instructor or facilitator with a teaching style like:

Mother Teresa's_____Attila the Hun's

2.   I learn best:

In a circus atmosphere_____In a churchlike setting

3.   In terms of lectures, I learn best:

In 2-minute knowledge bursts_____My attention span is like
                                                                                              the Energizer Bunny

4.   I typically relate to my fellow participants:

As if they were bubonic plaguettes_____As fellow picnickers in life's park

5.   I prefer curricular material:

That resembles a Congressional report_____That resembles the Cliff notes version

6.   In terms of overhead transparencies:

I'm reassured when the_____I prefer a natural delivery
instructor has organized
the course around them

7.   The course objectives:

Should be repeated often_____Are unnecessary; we know why we're here.

8.   I prefer breaks:

Every hour_____Decided by participants in response to Nature's calls

9.   Upon completion of a course, I typically:

Promise myself I'll use the material_____Teach others what I've learned

HANDOUT 26-2

Directions: The 15 items that follow reflect values associated with effective communications. Circle the number that indicates your opinion of how each value relates to your workplace.

1. *Goals*
vague, poorly defined   1   2   3   4   5   6   7   clearly stated

2. *Frequency of communications*
inadequate   1   2   3   4   5   6   7   sufficient

3. *Managers take us into their confidence*
no evidence of it   1   2   3   4   5   6   7   frequently

4. *Communications among coworkers*
hidden agendas   1   2   3   4   5   6   7   direct, honest

5. *Communications with our supervisors*
closed, dishonest   1   2   3   4   5   6   7   supportive, clear

6. *Interactions with customers*
often avoided   1   2   3   4   5   6   7   aligned with our job

7. *Benchmarking to improve via comparisons*
never heard of this   1   2   3   4   5   6   7   we engage in it

8. *Clarity of communications*
nonexistent   1   2   3   4   5   6   7   we understand expectations

9. *Length of communications*
excessive   1   2   3   4   5   6   7   clear and to-the-point

10. *Terms used*
I'm frequently lost   1   2   3   4   5   6   7   we understand the jargon

11. *Information needed*
is withheld   1   2   3   4   5   6   7   is shared

12. *Conflict*
threatens us   1   2   3   4   5   6   7   is properly handled

13. *Respect for the individual*
disrespect comes through   1   2   3   4   5   6   7   is quite evident

14. *Recognition of our efforts*
management doesn't care   1   2   3   4   5   6   7   management applauds us

15. *Trust*
we are not privy to   1   2   3   4   5   6   7   we are treated like adults
certain information we need

Total of 15 circled numbers: _____

Directions: Scoring information:

Calculate the total of all 15 circled numbers. If the assessment tool is used with coworkers, add all the individual totals and divide by the number of people in the work unit to obtain an average total score. Then obtain the average for each of the 15 items.

Scoring interpretation:

A.   An average score below 75 indicates the group as a whole is not communicating well. One way to overcome the problem is to determine which values are most critical and how those values could be shared or strengthened. The following activity will enable you and interested others to align individual values with group values and then to align those shared values with the goal the work unit is pursuing.

1.   Ask each person to select 5 of the 15 values most important to him or her. (There is no need to prioritize the items at this point.)

2.   Poll the group to learn which items were selected most often. Prioritize the top 3 choices.

3.   Brainstorm ways to increase the manifestation or practice of these 3 values.

4.   Develop an action plan to increase the likelihood of the most desired values serving as the foundation for future team meetings.

B.   For the individual items, those with an averaged group score of 4 or lower deserve special attention. These items could become serious problems for the work unit if not addressed. Outside help may be needed until the problems are resolved.

27

CAN YOU FIND THE PATTERN?

FORM

Those concerned with assuring quality have been trained to find recurring causes for certain effects. If we are unaware of the repetitive nature of those occurrences, we may misdiagnose the problem and misapply the solution. In this opener, participants have a chance to find reappearing patterns in numbers and letters, rather than in work processes or workplace conditions. They will work in small groups of four or five for about 10–15 minutes on this exercise.

FUNCTION

1. Divide the class into teams of four or five.

2. Distribute Handout 27-1. Give participants about 10 minutes to complete it.

3. Share the answers:

a) 11 (because the odd numbers are increasing by 2 each time) and 5 (because the even number, 10, goes down by one each time).

b) 1904, because two numbers are added together each time (8 + 10 = 18) and then multiplied by 2 to obtain the next number in the series (36). Next 36 is added to 10 to obtain 46, which is then doubled to obtain 92, and so on.

c) The letters represent the numbers 1 through 10, spelled out, so the next letter would be "N," for Nine.

d) 34, because every number is the added result of the preceding two numbers. (Fibonacci, a thirteenth-century Italian mathematician, analyzed numbers and discovered this interesting pattern among them.)

e) 20 would come next because the letters are alphabetically arranged: eighty, fifteen, forty, nineteen, one. So, twenty would come before two.

f) 134, because each number is doubled and then 6 is subtracted from it in order to find the next number.

g) 21, because each number is one-half the preceding number, plus 10.

4. Lead a discussion based on these questions:

a) In terms of positive occurrences in your workplace, what are some patterns that seem to be emerging?

b) In terms of negative occurrences in your workplace, what are some patterns that seem to be emerging?

c) What patterns, good or bad, seem to be occurring in your organization as a whole? In your industry? In the business world itself?

d) What is the value of contemplating emerging trends?

FOLLOW-UP

Collect other emerging pattern problems such as the following and use them to reinforce the need to pay attention to patterns as a means of preparing ourselves for the future.

Offer a token prize to the first student who is able to repeat this sequence (or write it on the board) without referring to notes:

105,989,184,777,063,564,942,352,821,147

Most participants will set right to work attempting to memorize the numbers when in fact there is a very powerful gimmick operating here: the numbers are organized in increments of 7. So all one really needs to do is remember where to end: at 105. Starting at the right with 7 and adding 7 each time will ultimately lead the prize winner to 105 (989, 184, 777, 063, 564, 942, 352, 821, 147).

Point out that data or information is not always organized so neatly for us but when it is, the recall process is considerably facilitated.

Recommend that participants read books such as *Megatrends 2000*, by John Naisbitt and Patricia Aburdene, or *TechnoTrends* by Daniel Burrus.

TRANSITION

Former Apple CEO John Sculley asserts, "The best way to be prepared for the future is to invent it." That invention, though, must be predicated on careful deliberation and analysis of patterns that seem to be emerging. Otherwise we may create something that has little value. In the knowledge you will acquire today and in the skills you will develop lie the seeds for future creations. You are, by virtue of continuous learning, preparing yourselves for eventualities that are definitely emerging. Take advantage of everything and everyone you can, in terms of preparing yourself intellectually for the future.

HANDOUT 27-1

Directions: See if you can discover the pattern among the combinations of numbers and letters in order to determine what comes next.

a)   1 10 3 9 5 8 7 7 9 6 ____ ____

b)   8 10 36 92 256 696 ____

c)   O T T F F S S E ____

d)   0, 1, 1, 2, 3, 5, 8, 13, 21, ____

e)   80, 15, 40, 19, 1   What comes next: 20 or 2? _____ Why? _____

f)   8, 10, 14, 22, 38, 70 ____

g)   36, 28, 24, 22, ____

If you finish ahead of the others, spend a few moments thinking about these questions:

a)   In terms of positive occurrences in your workplace, what are some patterns that seem to be emerging?

b)   In terms of negative occurrences in your workplace, what are some patterns that seem to be emerging?

c)   What patterns, good or bad, seem to be occurring in your organization as a whole? In your industry? In the business world itself?

d)   What is the value of contemplating emerging trends?

28

DEFINE AND SHINE

FORM

Mark Twain commented about the weather, "Everyone talks about it but no one does anything about it." If paraphrased, that thought could easily apply to certain words that are bandied about the work environment. Often, no one has ever stopped to define those words. As a result, there are multiple interpretations under which employees operate.

This opener has small groups define certain words to ensure everyone is reading from the same sheet of music. Although it takes about 10 minutes, this exercise will help establish the common ground in which knowledge seeds can sprout. The only equipment needed is a flip chart and marking pens.

FUNCTION

1. Divide the group into teams of three or four.

2. For about 2 minutes, ask the teams to come up with a list of five of the most important words related to the subject being presented. For example, if the class is focused on teambuilding, relevant words might be synergy, facilitator, agenda, improvement, and brainstorming.

3. Ask each team to tell you their words as you write them on the flip chart, eliminating duplicates.

4. Now select one word (the one you feel is most important) and place a star in front of it.

5. Have the teams define that word.

6. Call on each team to share its definition, supplementing each definition with course-relevant information of your own.

FOLLOW-UP

Suggest that participants take some of the terms defined in the workshop back to the work site and post them in a prominent place to invite further discussion and awareness among coworkers. For example, Dr. Deming often declared that "Quality is what the customer says it is." This is a reminder for those in the customer service business to learn as much as they can about customer preferences and how customers themselves would define the word *satisfaction*.

TRANSITION

For the sake of having a common understanding, let's use this as our operating definition of the word '_____.' [Supply the word you have starred on the flip chart and provide a definition using the input from the group] *As further discussions are held and as ideas and issues are presented, keep this definition in mind. As need dictates, we will continue to define other critical terms throughout the day.*

29

MEET ME IN THE MIDDLE

FORM

Within minutes, participants will join one of two groups, based on their assessments of the extent of knowledge they currently possess on the topic for which you are offering training. The middle group, the 3's, ideally can meet in a breakout room. Each group will prepare a report in about 10 minutes and then deliver it in 1–2 minutes.

FUNCTION

1. Ask participants to think about their current level of knowledge regarding the topic being presented. If they know next to nothing about the subject, have them write the number 1 or 2 on their papers. If this is a subject that has long interested them and in which they have done extensive reading, have them write a 4 or 5. If they have only an average or fair amount of knowledge on the subject, ask them to write a 3 on their papers.

2. Divide the class as follows:

First, have the 1s and 2s meet with the 4s and 5s for about 10 minutes. Their charge is this: The 4s and 5s will tell the 1s and 2s what they believe are the most important things the 1s and 2s should learn. The 1s and 2s on their part will ask questions, such as, "How has the learning you have acquired made your job easier?" or, "How long did it take you to learn all this?" A recorder will capture the essential points.

Ask the 3s to wait in a breakout room (or in the back of the training room if a breakout room is not available) while you explain the assignment to the others. When you have finished your brief instructions to the first group, meet with the 3s and give them this assignment: "Other than computer training, training programs have a historically poor record of effecting change in the workplace. Your task for the next ten minutes is to come up with a list of ways the people in this room can make best use of the training they are about to receive. Record your ideas, as you will be asked to make a brief report when the groups merge again."

3. Reassemble the entire group and have a spokesperson from the 1s and 2s and the 4s and 5s report the main points of their discussions. A spokesperson for the 3s will do the same.

FOLLOW-UP

Ask for volunteers to assume a leadership role in executing some of the projects suggested by the 3s team.

List the questions raised by the 1s and 2s on chart paper and as the answers come up during the natural course of training events, record them next to the questions on the chart paper.

TRANSITION

Each of you, even the 5s, should walk out of here at the end of the day with your knowledge level moved up a notch. Whether or not you do, of course, depends on your willingness to take a proactive role as a learner. Don't simply let the knowledge you are about to receive wash over you. Absorb it. Note it. Discuss it. Question it. Promise to do something with it.

30

A WORD FROM THE WISE

FORM

Participants will work individually to select a preferred quotation from the handout. Then, they will join three or four others to discuss their selections. Each team will next select one quotation, relate it to reasons for taking the course, and share this in a short report to the other members of the class. Altogether, the opener will take about 15 minutes.

FUNCTION

1. Distribute Handout 30-1 and ask participants to select the one quotation most meaningful to them.

2. Form teams of four or five. Ask each member, in an introductory gesture, to share his or her quotation and its significance with the team.

3. As a whole, the team will now select one quotation, relate it to the training they are about to receive, and prepare a simple report to be shared with the other teams.

4. Invite a spokesperson from each team to report on the team's selection and its relationship to training.

FOLLOW-UP

Suggest that each participant make a brief report at the next team or staff meeting, detailing what he or she has learned and its application to the work done in the business unit. The report should begin with a quotation that illustrates the relevance of the training to the work being done.

TRANSITION

Billy Graham has wisely observed that "hot heads and cold hearts never solved anything." Quotations such as his often set the tone for events taking place. For this training event, it is my fervent hope that you will combine cold heads (i.e., rational thought) and hot hearts (i.e., learning passion) to this course today.

Henry Ford:	*Coming together is a beginning. Keeping together is progress. Working together is success.*
Beca Lewis Allen:	*Yearn to understand first and be understood second.*
Donald Trump:	*I like thinking big. If you're going to be thinking anyway, you might as well be thinking big.*
Lyndon Johnson:	*There are no problems that we cannot solve together and very few that we can solve by ourselves.*
Lily Tomlin:	*I've always wanted to be somebody, but I see now that I should have been more specific.*
Charles M. Schultz:	*There is no greater burden than great potential.*
Henry Clay:	*Statistics are no substitute for judgment.*
Diane Ravitch:	*The person who knows "how" will always have a job. The person who knows "why" will always be the boss.*
Arthur Lenehan:	*After all is said and done, more is said than done.*
George Bernard Shaw:	*Progress is impossible without change, and those who cannot change their minds cannot change anything.*
Stirling Moss:	*To achieve anything, you must be prepared to dabble on the boundary of disaster.*
William Bulger:	*There is never a better measure of what a person is than what he does when he's absolutely free to choose.*
Peter Drucker:	*Systematic change requires a willingness to look on change as an opportunity.*
Conrad Hilton:	*Success seems to be connected with action.*
Liza Minelli:	*Reality is something you rise above.*
Anonymous:	*Most of us will never do great things, but we can do small things in a great way.*
Colin Powell:	*The healthiest competition occurs when average people win by putting in above-average effort.*
An Wang:	*Success is more a function of consistent common sense than it is of genius.*
Beverly Sills:	*You may be disappointed if you fail, but you are doomed if you don't try.*
Luther Standing Bear:	*Thought comes before speech.*

31

INTUIT AND OUT OF IT

FORM

Working in teams of six or seven, participants will soon be termed Intuits or Out-of-Its, as a result of their answers to the worksheet questions. This opener requires no advance preparation (other than making copies of the handout) and will take about 10 minutes for the teams to decide on their collective answers.

FUNCTION

1. Once teams of six or seven have been assembled, distribute Handout 31-1 and have the teams agree on their answers.

2. Give the answers, which are:

1— $747 million
2— 60%
3— 33
4— 98.3%
5— $13 trillion
6— 75%
7— 28%
8— 1916
9— 7 million
10— 1,900+ pounds

3. The team that had the highest number of correct answers will serve as the Intuits for the remainder of the day. Whenever questions arise to which you know the answer, ask the Intuits first what their prediction is.

Also determine which team had the lowest number of correct answers. They will be the Out-of-Its. Ask them, after you have asked the Intuits, what they think the answers would be for various issues that are raised. Keep a friendly competition going between the two groups.

FOLLOW-UP

Encourage participants to keep a log tracking all the significant work-related decisions they make during the course of the next month. They should indicate which of those decisions are based on intuition and which are based on statistics. Once the outcome of the decision has been ascertained, they should return to the log and record their degree of satisfaction with the results. In this way, they will have a good feel for the worth of their intuitive decisions.

TRANSITION

Actually, you will need very little intuitive ability to figure out the answers to the many questions I will be posing to you today. You will need, however, to work synergistically, to use the facts you already know and are about to learn, and to analyze likely outcomes.

Directions: As a team, decide on a number you feel would be the most accurate answer to each question.

1. Former Beatles star Paul McCartney is worth how much? _____

2. In 1970, 80% of adults read a newspaper every day of the week. Today, that percentage is _____.

3. In 1956, there were 94 cities that had two or more newspapers, owned by separate firms. How many such cities are there today? _____

4. What percentage of American homes have at least one television in them? _____

5. What is the amount of discretionary income and inheritances baby boomers and charities are expected to receive in the next 10 years? _____

6. What percentage of Fortune 100 companies have formal corporate vision or mission statements? _____

7. What percentage of Americans have not read a book in the last 6 months? _____

8. The first woman (Jeanette Rankin) was elected to Congress in what year? _____

9. For every one person on earth, there are _____ bugs.

10. How much garbage does the average American throw away in a given year?

32

META4, 4 U

FORM

Participants will work in two's or three's on this opener, which will take about 10 minutes for completion. First, they will discuss an impending change facing them (their team, their department, their organization, or their industry). Then, they will select an image from the worksheet that best conveys the essence of the change.

FUNCTION

    1.   Ask each person to find a partner(s) with whom he or she will work.

    2.   Now address the class as a whole and ask them, one at a time, to cite an impending change—one they themselves are facing, or one their team, their department, their organization, or their industry is facing.

    3.   Record the changes on the flip chart.

    4.   Share with the class the quotation from author Warren Bennis: "If I were to give off-the-cuff advice to anyone seeking to institute change, I would ask, 'How clear is your metaphor?'"

    5.   Distribute Handout 32-1 and ask the pairs to find an image that can serve as a metaphor for one of the changes listed on the flip chart.

    6.   Call on a few people to share their metaphoric perspectives on change.

FOLLOW-UP

Obtain copies of speeches (especially those delivered by CEOs) and have participants locate the metaphors in them.

    Collect business-related metaphors such as the following and lead a discussion concerning them:

> "[Organizational DNA] is the stuff, mostly intangible, that determines the basic character of a business."   —James F. Moore

> "At first glance, a quality-oriented business and an orchestra might not appear to have much in common."—Charles Hammons and Gary Maddux

> "We once hired a young man in our London office who turned out to be a genuine thoroughbred compared to his plowhorse boss."
>   —Mark McCormack

TRANSITION

By virtue of your presence in this training program, you are indicating your willingness to change—if only by adding to the contents of your knowledge banks. The material that will be presented to you today should change some of your attitudes, some of your outlooks, some of your approaches. In time, you will use your new knowledge to make changes to the work processes in which you engage. Here is a metaphor that should give you a sense of the big picture I'll be painting for you today. Let's consider this umbrella [Actually draw one on the flip chart] *as the curricular core of this program. Each of the spokes represents one of the instructional elements holding up that umbrella. This first spoke* [Write in the first objective or outline heading and continue until all the main points of the course have been equated with one of the umbrella spokes]....*

Directions: Working with one or two others, select one of the images below to illustrate one change listed on the flip chart. Then explain the significance of your selection, i.e., how does this image relate to the impending change?

This image is a metaphor for this change _____

because_____

_____

_____

_____

33

RACONTERSE

FORM

In *Management by Storying Around*, author David Armstrong asserts the need, as many have done before and since, for managers to use stories as an effective communications tool. After reviewing true and fictional stories on the handout, teams of four will share stories of their own and then vote on one to share with the class as a whole in order to illustrate how this training can impact their future actions. Plan on 10–15 minutes for completion of this exercise. (Storytellers are encouraged to be terse and not rambling raconteurs.)

FUNCTION

1. Divide the group into teams of four.

2. Distribute Handout 33-1.

3. After they have read it, ask each person to come up with an anecdote or true story of a work-related experience he or she has had. The experience should illustrate in some way how training can positively impact workplace relationships or workplace productivity.

4. Ask each team to decide which of the four stories they feel best illustrates the power of learning to alter behavior.

5. Preface the storytelling (to be delivered by one raconteur from each team) by reminding the group of the need for the stories to be told succinctly, tersely, and without rambling or irrelevant details.

6. Invite the storytellers, one at a time, to share their tales.

FOLLOW-UP

Author and former CEO Max DePree maintains that one of the signs of organizational atrophy occurs "when people stop telling tribal stories or cannot understand them." Encourage participants to begin collecting such tribal stories upon their return to the workplace as an anti-atrophy measure. Recommend DePree's book, *Leadership Is an Art*.

TRANSITION

Tribal stories often evolve from those defining moments that capture the essence of an individual or an organization, an event, or the quality philosophy behind a product or service. All of the stories I will tell you today are true stories. They underscore the points I will be making about _____ [Mention title of course]. I'll start with the story Philip Crosby tells about the time he was stopped in an airport by a young man, who Crosby assumed wanted his autograph. But he was wrong. Instead, the young man implored, "Please, Mr. Crosby, speak guru to me."

Mr. Crosby, rushing to catch a plane, facetiously replied, "Young man, do not rub Ben-Gay on every part of your body," and hurried off. I will not be speaking guru today either. As much as I know about this subject, I do not know all there is to know. Many of you have done reading and studying on your own. Please, share your knowledge with the rest of us. None of us, after all, is as smart as all of us.

1.   In the middle of a quiet lake on a placid afternoon, a fisherman was suddenly startled by a thumping on the side of his boat. He looked down and saw a water snake with a frog in its mouth. Knowing the frog's life was at stake but also knowing the snake was hungry, the fisherman decided food was the answer to both dilemmas. Unfortunately, the only thing he had on board was a bottle of bourbon, which he willingly poured down the snake's throat. All was well, the snake released the frog. Within 20 minutes, though, he heard an even louder thumping. He looked down again. This time, he saw the snake with *two* frogs in its mouth!

2.   Cordell Hull, an American statesman, was known for his measured speech and unwillingness to make assumptions. On a train one day, he and a friend were gazing out the window at the farm animals in the field. "Look," his friend noted, "those sheep have just been sheared."

Hull thought a moment and then remarked, "On this side, at least."

3.   Secretary of the Navy Knox was once asked by a friend to reveal information about ships in the Atlantic. Not wishing to sever the relationship but equally unwilling to divulge confidential information, he spoke conspiratorially: "Can you keep a secret?"

"Of course I can," came his friend's staunch reply.

"Well," replied the Secretary, "so can I."

4.   President Franklin Roosevelt was used to people becoming nervous in his presence—so nervous they often did not hear what he said to them. In a playful mood one day, he decided to give the same response to everyone going through the receiving line. When asked, "How are you, Mr. President?" Roosevelt replied, "Fine, thank you. I just murdered my mother-in-law!"

As expected, no one really heard him, for people shook his hand and mouthed inanities like, "I'm glad to hear it."

The Chinese ambassador, however, with finer listening skills than most, stopped in mid-bow with a confused look on his face. He straightened up and then politely remarked, "I'm certain she deserved it, sir."

5.   Trust is an integral element in business relationships. There are those, however, who trust only after they have established it is absolutely safe to do so. Such was the case with Marshall Field III, who approached an old, old woman in a hotel at the turn of the century. "Can you crack nuts?" he demanded to know.

"Heavens, no," she chuckled. "I lost all my teeth ages ago."

"Good," Field is reputed to have declared. He then extended two hands full of pecans and asked, "Please hold these while I go get more."

6.   In a clear example of monarchy adoration, an Englishman once remarked to an American, "How unpleasant it must be for you Americans to be governed by people whom one would never think of asking to dinner."

The American's retort was swift and unpretentious: "No more unpleasant," he asserted, "than being governed by people who wouldn't ask you to dinner."

7.   A boorish dinner guest, with very poor table manners, held up his fork with a piece of meat on it and demanded of his hostess, "Is this pig?"

She sweetly queried in return, "To which end of the fork are you referring?"

8.   An overbearing English lord remarked to James Whistler, "I passed your house this morning."

"Thank you," Whistler commented, "thank you very much."

34

DEFENSIVE LINES

FORM Football-related lines appear on the worksheet for this opener, which takes about 10 minutes to complete. Participants will work in teams of four to select one reference and relate it in some way to either the training they are undergoing, the work they do, or the workplaces where they do that work.

FUNCTION 1. Divide the group into teams of four and distribute Handout 34-1.

2. Allow about 8 minutes for teams to complete the assignment.

3. Ask each team to explain its selection.

FOLLOW-UP Collect comparable quotations from either sports, entertainment, or political figures and ask participants to relate them to their posttraining intentions to use what they have learned.

TRANSITION *Although this opener was a tongue-in-cheek look at some of the issues you face every day, the work that lies before us is quite serious. My job is to cover the material in the most efficient, meaningful way possible. Your job is to absorb as much as you can and to use it afterwards. Please, if anything I've said is not clear, ask me about it. I promise not to become defensive.*

HANDOUT 34-1

Directions: Study these lines about defensive linemen. (It doesn't matter whether you follow the game of football.) Next, working with three others, select one of the lines and tell how it relates to the training you are receiving, or to the work you do, or to the places where you work.

1. "Sacks are garbage stats. One guy does all the work, and the other one gets the sack." (Joe Galat, Houston Oilers coach)

2. "At halftime, I told the coach my deepest secrets. I said I never wanted to be buried at sea, I never wanted to get hit in the mouth with a hockey puck, and I didn't want to go out and play that second half against Lee Roy Selmon." (Ted Albrecht, Chicago Bears)

3. "When he [William, the Refrigerator, Perry] goes into a restaurant, he doesn't ask for a menu; he asks for an estimate." (Tony Kornheiser, sportswriter)

4. "Merlin Olsen went swimming in Loch Ness—and the monster got out." (Jim Murray, sportswriter)

5. "Merlin Olsen is very big, very strong, has great speed and great agility, is a very smart ballplayer, gives at least 110 percent on every play, and those are his weak points." (Jerry Kramer, Green Bay Packers)

6. "He's like Felix Unger, a total neat freak. He keeps his cereal boxes in alphabetical order." (Lisa Gastineau, speaking of husband Mark)

7. "You could try to block [Fred] Dean with a pickup truck, and it wouldn't work. He's too good, too fast, and no rules committee is ever going to stop him." (Pat Haden, Los Angeles Rams quarterback)

8. "He [Elvin Bethea, Houston Oilers] doesn't get hurt. He's a hurter, not a hurtee." (Bum Phillips, Houston Oilers coach)

9. "He [Coy Bacon, Los Angeles Rams] is a fern brain—if he had any less of an IQ, he would be a plant in a botany class." (Stan Walters, Philadelphia Eagles offensive tackle)

ENERGIZERS

35

TRI-DENTS

FORM

Working in small groups of four or five, participants will take 5–10 minutes to create three-word sentences that capture what they have learned for the past hour or what new perspectives (angles) they have acquired since the session began, what new dents have been made on their gray matter. No special equipment is needed other than paper and pencils. If flip charts are available, groups can use them to record their favorite try-angles.

FUNCTION

1.   Divide the class into small groups.

2.   Introduce the assignment in this way:

Throughout history, we have been inspired by three-word phrases that capture the memory of events too significant to forget—Remember the Maine or Remember Pearl Harbor. Just as triangles are figures not easily weakened, so are tri-word phrases not easily forgotten. In more recent times, we have quality advocates such as Dr. Joseph Juran telling us to "Eliminate turf wars," or Dr. Deming telling us to "Drive out fear." We even have Sam Walton advising that we "Eliminate the dumb." The popular Hollywood line—Lights, camera, action—is similar to the childish exhortation—Ready? Set? Go! Even advertisers recognize the strength of the tri-worded phrases that encourage us to try: "Just do it" is the most familiar of all.

Today I'm going to give you about five minutes to work in groups and come up with at least five three-word phrases that reflect what we have been discussing and learning about this morning. [Give examples to reflect the instructional focus. A class on leadership, for example, might have covered the fact that "Leaders take risks." Or a session on empowerment might lead to "Empowerment means initiative."] Are there any questions?

3.   Once the allotted time is up, ask each group to select their favorite phrase and record it on the flip chart. Then call on each team to briefly share their favorite.

Ask for a volunteer to collect all the try-angles that have been created throughout the training program and to type them up for distribution to all class members and their supervisors. The volunteer may also choose to send out one e-mail message each week to the class attendees as a reinforcer of concepts acquired. The message should encourage participants to discuss the try-angled concepts with coworkers.

TRANSITION

It's important to stop periodically and review what's been covered. Doing so increases the likelihood that you are encoding the most salient points from the instruction in your mental storage banks. If we fail to do this, the knowledge strands tend to run together like strands of spaghetti on a plate.

We've heard some excellent three-word review statements here. Now let me give you one of mine: "Let's move on!"

36

FORCED FITS

A mid-session energizer, this activity has participants work in groups of three or four to think back over the material presented from the beginning of the session to this point. They will then decide on the most valuable concept they have learned so far, but…they must express that concept in a forced-fit expression. The exercise takes about 10 minutes to complete and requires no special equipment or material.

FUNCTION

1. Divide the group into teams of three or four.

2. Ask teams to discuss what they have learned so far. Then, as a team, they will decide which concept or skill they feel is the most important of all those presented thus far.

3. They will then express that concept within a forced fit. The choices are:

   a) L-M-N-O-P   This structure requires them to write a sentence of only five words. The first word must start with an "l," the second with an "m," the third with an "n," the fourth with an "o," and the last with a "p." For example, in a communications class, the L-M-N-O-P sentence might be: "Levity might negate officious pomposity."

   b) 1-2-3-4   Somehow, the numbers must be related to the content of the course. To illustrate, in a class on empowerment, the structure might be: "*One* thing that we must remember is our own power to lead. *Two* quotations will help: General Patton's comment that we need to give direction, not directions; and the IBM motto: 'If you build fences around people, you get sheep.' *Three* authorities who have written about empowerment are Peter Block, Tom Peters, and Max DePree. *Four* steps to empowering yourself include Learning, Experimenting, Gathering Support, and Maintaining Enthusiasm."

4. Ask each team to share its forced-fit expression.

FOLLOW-UP

Periodically, give the same assignment, but change the letters to any combination of five.

Collect the forced-fit comments, type them up, and share them with future classes.

TRANSITION

I hope you've enjoyed this exercise and that it made you stretch. In a larger sense, this training is designed to make you stretch as well. The next concept I will present, in fact, is quite complicated. Take careful notes but do not hesitate to tell me if and when I've lost you.

37

EACH ONE TEACH ONE

FORM

A good change-of-pace activity, this energizer asks participants to reflect on one idea that has truly sunk in—a bit of knowledge, a formula, a technique, et cetera they have fully comprehended. They then teach that idea to a partner, who in turn teaches his or her own concept. The exercise takes about 10 minutes and requires no materials other than a flip chart and marking pen.

FUNCTION

1.   Divide the group into teams of five or six and ask each team, without looking at their notes (or anyone else's notes), to write down the 10 or 15 most important things they have learned thus far.

2.   Ask each person in each team to isolate the one kernel of information they most fully understand.

3.   Mix up the teams now: Have each participant find someone on another team as his or her partner. The partners will then teach each other the knowledge kernels they have selected.

FOLLOW-UP

Suggest participants serve as SMEs (subject matter experts) when they return to the workplace and that they teach coworkers at least one of the skills they have learned in this training.

TRANSITION

The goal, of course, is to have you feel as comfortable with all the major concepts as you feel with the one you have selected. How can I help you? What is still unclear to you? What should I repeat, more clearly, more carefully this time?

38

AND THE PARAPHRASE GOES TO...

FORM

Fun, creativity, and serious review come together in this energizer, which will take small groups of four or five about 10 minutes to complete. It begins with the class taking stock of the major points made thus far. Then, teams will select one of the main ideas and express it using the speaking styles of individuals listed on the transparency.

FUNCTION

1. Elicit from class members a list of the major concepts presented to this point that stand out in their minds. At least ten should be recorded on the flip chart. (Note: If they overlook some points you feel are integral to the curriculum, add them to the list.)

2. Form teams of four or five and ask each team to select one idea.

3. Then show Transparency 38-1 and ask the teams to express their selection from the various perspectives of the individuals listed on the transparency. For example, in response to a question about the causes of or solutions for stress, we might have:

David Letterman:	"And the No. 1 reason—being understaffed!"
Bob Dylan:	"And the answer, my friend, is showing in the din."
Mae West:	"Handling multiple priorities ain't for sissies!"
Jimmy Durante:	"Good nights—with your mister or missus—wherever you are."
William F. Buckley:	"The salient solution, it appears to me, is the conversion of simple stress to eustress, a solution effected through the manifestation of multiplicative gestures that are seemingly insignificant when looked at in isolation but that, incrementally, are cumulative—even multiplicative—in their ultimate outcome."
Robert Frost:	"Two requests converged in a busy office, and I, I took the one less difficult to complete."

4.   Call on a spokesperson from each team to share paraphrases of the idea they selected.

FOLLOW-UP
Have the same groups use the flip chart list to write an article about these concepts, which are not now listed in any particular order. The article, however, should have a logical flow among the concepts and should make use of transitions to connect the ideas.

Have the articles published in the organizational newsletter.

TRANSITION
I hope you've had some fun with these paraphrases. But don't overlook these concepts, which are critical to your understanding of this topic and important for the application of these concepts to the work you do.

Bill Cosby

President Clinton

Eleanor Roosevelt

Muhammad Ali

Tiger Woods

Isaac Asimov

Madonna

Erma Bombeck

Aretha Franklin

Sigmund Freud

General Patton

Miss Piggy

Donald Trump

Other:

39

AND THE AWARD GOES TO...

FORM

At low points during the training day when spirits are starting to sag, reenergize the group wth this activity, which places them in groups of five or six, charged with the responsibility of selecting one of their own members to receive an award. The name of the award will depend on what has transpired thus far in class. So, if one person always had his or her hand up whenever you were looking for a volunteer, that person might receive the Volunteer of the Year or Most Likely to Succeed award. If someone in the group is an assiduous notetaker or always serves as recorder, he or she might receive the Amazing Amanuensis award. Teams will also prepare a short presentation speech, using the handout information to assist them.

This energizer takes about 15 minutes; its effectiveness is heightened if you can purchase several inexpensive trophies in advance for teams to award to various individuals. If this is not possible, have certificates available for the teams to fill in.

FUNCTION

1. Divide the class into teams of five or six.

2. Explain that you have been so satisfied with the effort they have put into content mastery that you think it would be appropriate at this point to recognize participants' contributions. Except...you want each team to decide on one person to receive an award. Each team, then, will look over the other participants and identify one person who has been outstanding in some positive way. They will decide on the name of the award they wish to present.

3. Ask teams to notify you as soon as they have decided on the person and the name of the award. When they do so, give each team member a copy of Handout 39-1 and ask them to prepare a short presentation speech to accompany the awarding of the trophy or certificate to the honoree.

4. Ask each team to make its presentation.

FOLLOW-UP

Ask each recipient to prepare an acceptance speech. (As they are doing so, preview the content for the remainder of the session. Or, ask the teams to decide on the five most important things they have learned thus far. Then have each team call on another team to explain one of the five things they have listed.) After 5–6 minutes, have the recipients stand and deliver their acceptance speeches.

TRANSITION

For those of you who did not receive an award—and that means most of us sitting here—realize you are unacknowledged recipients of the Susan Lucci Perseverance Award. Winners like you are willing to carry on, determined to work hard and do your best, even though your peers have failed to recognize your efforts. There will be a reward for you, though. By virtue of your commitment to learning as much this afternoon as you have learned this morning, you will come out ahead—in your jobs, in your lives, and certainly in your own self-confidence. Carry on, Lucci-ites, carry on.

When giving or receiving an award or making an actual speech, your opening words and closing remarks are especially important. The former help the audience decide if you are worth listening to. The latter help them decide if you were worth remembering.

The elements of effective openings are the very same elements that constitute effective closings. Fortunately, there is a wide array of possibilities from which to choose. The following are techniques for capturing the audience's interest—either because they are the first words they hear or the last. If well-prepared, these openings and closings will evoke admiration.

If you were to prepare a speech on creativity, for instance, instead of a speech to present (or accept) an award, the following methods could be used:

Quotations	*"Bring ideas in," Mark Van Doren said, "and entertain them royally, for one of them may be the king."*
Statistics	*Seven out of ten adults in a recent survey labeled themselves as not very creative.*
Illustration	*Anyone can acquire knowledge. Using the knowledge we have acquired—now that is a different matter altogether. Even Albert Einstein admitted that imagination is more important than knowledge.*
Anecdote	*A 29-year-old artist named Peter Laird drew a turtle with a mask and numchucks. He borrowed $700, combined it with a $500 tax refund, and printed 3,000 copies of a black and white comic book. Within a few years, he headed a billion-dollar empire, with Ninja Turtles at its core.*
Definition	*"Imagineering" is the process of using your imagination to engineer a totally new concept.*
Comparison	*Using your imagination is a lot like solving a math problem, as we have seen.*
Contrast	*Engineers deal in logic. Artists, by comparison, deal with intuition and whimsy.*
Audio or visual effects	*Listen to this music for just a moment. [Pause.] This is the result of a musician's search for the creative force within. That same force resides within each of us as well. Today, we've learned how to tap into that force. Tomorrow, ideally, you will remember this music and remember your own creative potential.*
Gimmick	*This Energizer battery is like your imagination—it just keeps going and going and going. Remember, as long as you are alive, you will be able to imagine new possibilities.*

40

M PROMPT: U

FORM

This energizer depends on M words as prompts for impromptu speeches. Each person in a small group of five or six draws a word from an envelope and then relates the word to the training being conducted. It will take about 10 minutes for each team to complete its rounds, and about 15 minutes if the teams are willing to share one of the M-prompt speeches. In advance of this exercise, make copies of Handout 40-1, one sheet per team. Cut out the words on each sheet and place them in an envelope (one envelope per team).

FUNCTION

1. Divide the class into teams of five or six.

2. Deliver this mini-lecture:

It was Mark Twain who commented, "It usually takes me more than three weeks to prepare a good impromptu speech." Unfortunately, in the business world, we seldom have advance warning that we will be called upon to deliver a few remarks. Although Twain's words were intended to be tongue-in-cheek, there are things we can do to ensure our impromptu speeches receive good marks, whether they are delivered informally in a staff meeting or classroom or more formally in a conference, interview, or media situation. Today, you will have an opportunity to sharpen your thinking-on-your-feet skills.

3. Give an envelope to one person in each team. Ask him or her to withdraw an M word and to use it as a prompt for structured comments related to the training being conducted (or to ways of applying the training). Use this example for the M-prompt, Media.

The media have reported over and over again how valuable conflict resolution skills are. Just this morning I read an article about the Hagberg Consulting Group, which found those managers who were in trouble were the ones who were unable to iron out the wrinkles in relationships—their own and others'. Last week, I read an article about Don Petersen, former CEO of Ford Motor Company, who was quoted as saying, "Results depend on relationships." What we are learning about conflict resolution is helping me quite a bit, even though I'm not a man-

ager. It is making me realize that if I can manage myself, the rest comes pretty easily.

4.   When the first person finishes, the envelope is passed to the next person in the team and the process continues until each person has had an opportunity to share his or her thoughts.

5.   Note that you overheard some pretty interesting comments as you were circulating around the room; express the hope that some teams would be willing to share their presentations with the class as a whole. (Ideally, some hands will go up.) Call on a few volunteers.

FOLLOW-UP

Divide the class into triads. One person turns to a second person and asks, "Could you tell me your thoughts about _____?" (Any suitable topic could be used.) The third person makes notes on how effectively the second person presented his or her impromptu remarks. Once the speaker has finished, the observer shares his or her insights and a new rotation begins. By the end of the exercise, each member of the triad will have had an opportunity to be the topic selector, the impromptu-remarks speaker, and the observer.

Make prompts for other letters of the alphabet and periodically have participants deliver other impromptu speeches.

TRANSITION

In a sense, we are all in here today because we are seeking ways to enhance our careers. According to Lee Iacocca, "The best thing you can do for your career is learn to think on your feet." While we could never anticipate every verbal challenge that lies before us, we can practice the skill of being able to express our thoughts even when we have not had much time for preparation. When you return to your jobs, your supervisor and perhaps even your coworkers are bound to have questions for you concerning the training in which you participated today. Continue to take good notes, to discuss the ideas presented, to ask questions, and periodically, to organize the volumes of information you are taking in, in a way that makes sense to you.

HANDOUT 40-1

manager	model
money	merger
measure	maverick
method	marketing
mandatory	material
morale	mission
mistake	meeting
many-sided	meaning

41

THAT'S DEBATABLE

FORM

As hotly contested issues arise during the course of the training day, keep a flip chart list of them. At some point in the last few hours of the session, one of those issues will be debated. The typical time frame for the debate itself is an hour; however, the format, as shown on the handout, has been reduced to 15 minutes. Another 10 minutes will be needed for preparation prior to the actual delivery and 5 minutes for the rebuttal preparation. (Have 3 x 5-inch cards available for the teams as they prepare.)

FUNCTION

1.   Introduce the activity this way:

Debating offers the opportunity to match wits with others and to create strong and memorable opinions, such as those Lincoln used in his debate against Douglas: "A house divided against itself cannot stand." Debates typically present opposing views on important issues, although the debates can be both formal and informal. Typically, in the workplace, debates are informal in nature. However, the organization of a formal debate can help to clarify issues that affect us, strategic plans that have to be made, and decisions awaiting resolution.

The issues around which debates are developed are called propositions; they are stated affirmatively. Examples might be, "The customer is always right," or, "Self-directed work teams should be leaderless," or, "Empowerment requires giving people both authority and responsibility."

2.   Divide the class into two teams.

3.   Announce that you will serve as judge. (If possible, invite another person, an outsider, to serve as a second judge.) Acknowledge that debaters ordinarily have the luxury of time—time to research and to develop their arguments. But, because participants are engaged in training today and not a presidential debate, they will only be allowed 10 minutes to organize their thoughts.

4.   Distribute Handout 41-1 and the 3 x 5-inch cards and tell them to get started.

5.   After 10 minutes, begin the debate.

6. Declare the winner and give reasons for your decision.

FOLLOW-UP Obtain videotapes of great debates, including political ones, and analyze them for effectiveness.

Invite two local politicians from opposing parties to conduct a debate for the class. Choose a topic such as affirmative action that has relevance for ordinary citizens as well as for employees.

TRANSITION

My compliments to you, to all of you. The kind of analytical thinking displayed in this debate is exactly what we need when we debate controversial issues at work or when we encounter resistance to ideas we feel are so evidently beneficial. When you return to work and begin to implement the ideas discussed here or begin to use the skills you have developed, some of you may encounter a few coworkers responding negatively to the changes you are proposing. Then, you will find that being able to marshal the facts to support your opinions, as you have done in this debate, is a valuable persuasion tool.

HANDOUT 41-1

1.	No matter what the proposition, the debating procedure remains the same. There is an equal number of debaters on each side. Those who argue in favor of the proposition are called the affirmative team. Those who argue against the proposition are known as the negative team.

2.	Team members spend time researching the topic. They try to find evidence that reflects the strongest possible arguments for proving their case. (A case consists of a set of reasons, arguments, supporting facts, and other evidence presented in favor of or against a proposition.) It helps to quote respected authorities if you can. Research should include the details that the opposing teams will probably use in their argument.

3.	Remember that in debating, opinions count for little. Without backup data, you are just another person with an opinion, as they say. Students should use 3 x 5-inch cards and should cite the *exact* sources from which they are quoting, rather than make notes about their own opinions. (Of course, in a training situation, you may not be able to do this, especially not in 10 minutes.)

4.	The debate has two phases. First is the opening statement, during which one or two persons from each team present the strongest arguments within the time allowed (usually twenty minutes for each side in an actual debate, but 5 minutes today for each team). Fifteen minutes are typically allotted following opening statements, although today you will only be allowed 5 minutes. During this time, the teams prepare their rebuttals.

The second phase, then, is the actual rebuttal, which is the other team's opportunity to respond to the opening statement. The rebuttal period is shorter, usually only 10 minutes for each side. Today's debate, however, allows 1½ minutes for the first rebuttal and 1 minute for the second rebuttal for each team. The stages, truncated for our purposes, are divided as follows:

First affirmative speech:	2½ minutes
First negative speech:	2½ minutes
Second affirmative speech:	2½ minutes
Second negative speech:	2½ minutes
First negative rebuttal:	1½ minutes
First affirmative rebuttal:	1½ minutes
Second negative rebuttal:	1 minute
Second affirmative rebuttal:	1 minute

5.	The judge then announces who won the debate on the basis of these criteria:

    a.	The strengths and weaknesses of the arguments

    b.	How well the challenged arguments are answered

    c.	The errors in evidence and reasoning that are pointed out or ignored by either team

    d.	The effectiveness of the delivery

Note that good listening skills are especially important for debaters. So is the ability to think quickly on one's feet. To illustrate: A lawyer once asserted in court that a corporation could not make an oral contract because a corporation has no tongue. The judge quickly reduced the argument to absurdity (the Latin expression for this is "reductio ad absurdum") by declaring that a corporation could not create a written contract either, because it has no hand.

42

PAINT-THE-TRAINER

FORM

This energizer requires participants to draw a sketch of you, and then to do their own psychological interpretations of their sketches, using handout pointers. Allow about 5 minutes for the exercise (and for the chuckles that are invariably produced). If possible, have a supply of markers available for participants.

FUNCTION

1. Ask participants to take out a clean sheet of paper and a pen or pencil.

2. Instruct them to draw a sketch of you. (If they ask for specifics, simply say it is their picture and they can draw it any way they wish.)

3. Tell them they can show their drawings to a partner if they wish to do so.

4. Distribute Handout 42-1. (Note: It heightens the humorous effect to have you read the information aloud, pausing as appropriate so participants can comment on the results to others, intoning as needed, making side—not snide—comments as you observe their reactions.)

FOLLOW-UP

Obtain a book about Rorschach tests from the library or a bookstore (*The Rorschach* by John Exner, for example). Ask for a volunteer to skim it at lunchtime (or overnight if the course lasts longer than day) and then to present a brief report to the class.

Get a copy of Ernest Dichter's book (*How Hot a Manager Are You?*) and use some of the exercises from it.

TRANSITION

Although we've had some fun with this exercise, it is based on a psychological truth, one that is perhaps best captured in the popular saying, "Every time you open your mouth or put words on paper [sketches, in this case], you permit others to see inside your brain."

For example, this is just one sentence from an actual job application form. The question was, "Why did you leave your last job?" The answer given: "They made me a scapegoat, just like my previous three employers did." One sentence—but probably enough for you to decide whether you would hire this person.

Although in a classroom situation no one is really analyzing your words—or your sketches—there are numerous other situations in which a single word can have powerful consequences. (In some companies, for example, if the word "we" is never heard during the employment interview, the applicant is not offered the job.) When you return to work, others will be paying very careful attention to what you say and how you say it (or draw it). To help create the kind of change-receptive environment in which new ideas can flourish—like the new ideas you are learning here—you will want to select your words and actions carefully. Otherwise, you may be revealing more than you wish to reveal—as some of you did with the drawings you made of me!

1. *Did you use any of the colored marking pens?* Yes☐ No☐

If so, there is a strong likelihood that you are the sort of person who appreciates excitement in the job, who likes challenges, who shuns routine.
If not, you are probably a meat-and-potatoes, salt-of-the-earth kind of person, one who likes to have everything in its place and who can stick to a job until it is finished.

2. *Do my legs appear in your drawing?* Yes☐ No☐

If so, you are quite a secure person, able to make a commitment and stick to it. You may even have been called stubborn.
If not, you are probably a continuous improvement kind of person—at least as far as your personal goals are concerned. You are not hesitant to make major changes in your life.

3. *Did you show my face looking left?* Yes☐ No☐

If so, you can be characterized as a thoughtful person, one who tries every day to make at least one person happier than he or she was before seeing you. You tend to be traditional and some-what conservative.

4. *Did you show my face looking right?* Yes☐ No☐

If so, you are probably known as the creative type, the sort of person who may appear scattered to others but who is exhilarated by taking an active and proactive response to possibilities.

5. *Did you show my face looking straight ahead?* Yes☐ No☐
If so, you probably play the role of devil's advocate on a fairly regular basis. You do not fear con-troversy. While you are loyal, you also do not hesitate to challenge those practices you regard as wasteful or downright foolish. You speak up when others cower in corners.

6. *Did you place the drawing in the upper left-hand corner?* Yes☐ No☐

If so, you could be described as the sort of person who both sees good in people and situations and who creates good in other people and situations. You do not hesitate to give to others—so much so that you may be taken advantage of on occasion.

7. *Did you place the drawing in the upper right-hand corner?* Yes☐ No☐

If so, others probably describe you as a patient and flexible person, one who can work well in vir-tually any setting, with virtually any kind of person.

8. *Did you place the drawing in the lower left-hand corner?* Yes☐ No☐

If so, you tend to be impatient. You may not be driving in the fast lane of line but you do enjoy being a passenger when someone else is driving. You don't like to be bogged down by people or things that deter you from your main mission in life.

9. *Did you place the drawing in the lower right-hand corner?* Yes☐ No☐

If so, that is a strong indication of an artistic nature, a sensitivity to color and balance, a desire for visual and auditory harmony. You are likely to enjoy music, poetry, and the performing arts.

10. *Did you place the drawing in the middle of the page?* Yes☐ No☐

If so, you are probably admired for your flexibility, your adaptability, your willingness to deviate from conventional paths.

11. *Are my ears visible?* Yes☐ No☐

If so, there is a strong possibility that you are an extremely good listener, reflecting an innate sensitivity to the feelings of other people. You hear the subtleties that are sometimes not even expressed. As a result, you have probably developed more friendships and strong working relationships than most people do.

12. *Is either of my arms raised?* Yes☐ No☐

If so, leadership potential is indicated. Accompanying this trait are the related traits of being energetic, persuasive, hardworking, and committed to a cause larger than everyday concerns.

13. *Is either of my hands open?* Yes☐ No☐

If so, not surprisingly, two personality traits are suggested. The first is a generous nature. You probably make regular donations to at least one charity, in addition to the money you give if you are in a place of worship. The second indication is of an open and trusting nature. You are less prone to suspicion than the average person.

14. *Beyond the basic body outline, are more than two details shown?* Yes☐ No☐

If so, you are a realistic, experienced individual, probably with many years on the job. You are not easily fooled and are seldom described as naive. People rely on you in crisis situations, for you are not easily unnerved. Rather, you are levelheaded and not swayed by excessive emotion.

If not, there is revealed an inclination to take risks. There is a possible danger, though, in your risk-taking ventures—you do not always research the situation as carefully as you should before embarking on your journeys into the unknown and untried.

15. *Did you draw any waves or curls or curves at all in my hair?* Yes☐ No☐

If so, you are probably very happy with the physical aspects of your relationship(s). (We are not referring to jogging partners here.)

If not, your romantic interludes, by these indications, are not as satisfying to you as other aspects of your life and job are.

43

THE SIXTY-SECOND INTERVIEW

FORM

This energizer has participants working in groups of six or seven (with one person serving as the timekeeper, who will keep a tally of all the seconds lost). Participants interview each other regarding the new knowledge they are acquiring and how they intend to use it. Have seven token prizes available for the team with the best time. All told, this activity takes about 10 minutes. The only preparation is to make copies of the handout questions, one for each team, and to cut them into strips. Place each set of questions into an envelope.

FUNCTION

1. Divide the class into teams of six or seven. (It is important that each team have the same number of team members. If any participants are left over, they can serve as roving observers, listening for responses they felt were especially significant. These responses can then be shared with the class as a whole upon completion of the exercise.)

2. Appoint one person in each team the timekeeper. His or her job will be to note how many seconds elapse (for each member of the team) between the time the person receives his or her question and the time he or she begins to speak.

3. Give each team an envelope. Ask one person in each team to begin by withdrawing a question. Before he or she reads it to the person to his or her left, you should explain that the recipient of the question should answer the question as quickly as possible—ideally with no hesitation at all.

4. Ask the timekeeper if he or she is ready to start the timing. If so, have the person with the question read it to the person beside him or her and have the timekeeper note how many seconds elapsed before the second person actually began responding to the question.

5. When every person on the team has had a chance to speak, ask which team had the winning score (the lowest total number of pre-speaking seconds). Award token prizes.

FOLLOW-UP

Ask each group to select one idea they intend to pursue once the training program is complete. Have a volunteer leader from each team pledge to contact the team members in 3 weeks to learn if they have actively pursued their public pledges. Have each volunteer then report the results to you. You will prepare a brief summary detailing whether the intentions were realized and share the summary with participants (and possibly with their supervisors if they give you permission to do so).

Invite members of the Human Resources or Personnel Departments to discuss the elements that constitute excellence in interview situations.

Collect articles about the need for good communication skills. For the next class session, give a different article to each participant and have them form pairs. Each person will teach his or her partner something he or she learned from the article. Then, the partner will do the same.

TRANSITION

There was a time in American work life when an employee would have an interview for initial entry into a company and would be set for [work] life—at least as far as further interviews were concerned. The days of womb-to-tomb employment, however, are long gone for the average employee. Even if one were to stay with the same organization until retirement, it is quite likely that interviews would be required for promotions, for membership on teams, and even for assignment to special projects.

To be sure, the training you are receiving will give you the confidence to speak knowledgeably on such occasions. The more skilled we are at responding quickly and knowledgeably, the better we can handle ourselves—whether we are being interviewed for a position in our own company or in another company or even being interviewed by a member of the media. In all interview circumstances, the more practice we've had with opening our mouths and not inserting our feet, the more professional we will appear.

1.   How do you intend to use the training you are receiving?

2.   If you had designed this training program, what would you have done differently?

3.   What has been the most interesting part of the day so far?

4.   What motivates you to be the ideal student?

5.   What will you share with your supervisor as far as this training program is concerned?

6.   What have you learned that you can use as soon as you return to work?

7.   Why do you think less than half the people who receive training make full use of it?

8.   What do you think of this training so far?

9.   In what ways are you as a adult learner like or different from the learner you were in high school?

10. Would you consider doing some training on this topic yourself? Why or why not?

11. How could you make use of current technology to extend the effectiveness of the training you are receiving?

12. If you were in charge of your organization, what training would you make mandatory for all employees?

13. What training do you feel all managers should have?

14. If you were writing the script for a video on the same topic as this training program, what would you put into the script?

15. Which businessperson do you most admire? How do you think he or she would teach this course?

44

S-TEAMS

FORM

After hearing a brief lecture about S-curves, teams of five or six will develop a letter theory of their own to explain how learning occurs. Including the time spent on reports from each team, this energizer will take about 15 minutes.

FUNCTION

1. Deliver the following mini-lecture:

The S-curve is actually a graph that shows the connection between the effort expended to learn something new and the results of those efforts. Obviously, our first encounter with new knowledge is often difficult and time-consuming. For example, just think about how long it took you, as a child, to learn to write your name. Compare that first encounter with the speed with which you now execute that same skill.

The S-curve resembles the letter S. [Draw the following on the flip chart.]

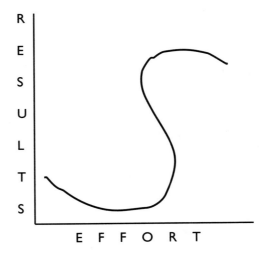

The plotting of the two variables typically produces a line that looks like an elongated S. On the lower left, we can see that progress is very slow. It will take some time before we will see results from the investment of time, energy, and resources. But once we have mastered the process and learned from our early mistakes, the payoff occurs very rapidly.

When we reach the top of the S-curve, though, we discover that the results begin to level off. This is explained by the fact that, given current bionic limitations, only certain achievements are possible within given standards. While as a kindergarten student it might have taken you thirty seconds to print your name and you can now do it in five, chances are that as hard as you work at it, you will probably not be able to reduce the time element much beyond the twenty-five-second reduction already achieved.

2. Divide the class into teams of five or six.

3. Give them this task:

Your job now is to come up with a cognitive principle of your own. In other words, "How do people learn?" You must, however, be able to express your ideas by way of a letter of the alphabet. Be ready, when called upon, to explain your theory.

4. After 10 minutes or so, ask each team to report.

FOLLOW-UP

Ask for other alphabetic references used in the world of business, such as playing your A game, attending one of the B schools, managing according to Theories X, Y, and Z, and so on. (You may even wish to include acronyms, such as MBWA [management by walking around], WIFM [What's in it for me?] and NIMBY [Not in my back yard].)

Lead a discussion centering on other examples of S-curves, not only for the individual participants, but for their organization, their industry, and the technology used to conduct business in both.

TRANSITION

During the first few minutes of this training session, you were probably overloading your learning circuits because of all the questions you had about the course and how it would be conducted, questions about me and about your fellow learners. Add to this cerebral chaos a little bit of nervousness due to a new situation and some awkwardness at being among strangers and you'll find your learning efficiency simply was not as good at the beginning as it is now. Now, you are familiar with my expectations, you know you can depend on your colleagues here, and you have a good idea of what the course content is.

In short, your S-curve really is starting to curve upward; the actual learning process has become more facile, the concepts are beginning to tie together. And speaking of concepts, the next one we are going to study deals with... [Mention name of next instructional module or next item on the course outline].

45

DELPHIAN DELIBERATIONS

FORM

The ancient Greeks created a method that permits honest input to delicate or controversial issues without requiring any one person to feel vulnerable because of such exposure. Participants respond anonymously to a question pertinent to the training content or context. Their written replies are then collected and the appointed facilitator leaves the room to prepare a synthesis. The whole exercise takes about 10 minutes (not counting the facilitator's analysis and subsequent report to the class).

FUNCTION

1.   During the course of the training day, keep a list of discussion points that led to some degree of friction or issues that generated strong opinions—ideally ones directly related to the work participants do or to the training subject itself. The list might also include problems that have arisen.

2.   From your observations of participants, select one person to serve as the facilitator. He or she should be someone who is articulate yet diplomatic, and someone whom the others seem to like and trust.

3.   Select one item from your list (ideally one that is pertinent to the training topic and that warrants further examination) and pose it to the group this way:

> *Often, controversial issues need to be discussed in order to be resolved. And yet, because of the deep feelings people hold on such issues, the very discussion can cause considerable division among those with opposing points of view. The Delphi Technique, thousands of years old, permits input without dissension; it invites involvement without running the risk of further controversy. I'd like you to give some serious thought now to an issue [concern, problem, point] that arose earlier today. We did not resolve the issue then, but perhaps we can now.*

4.   Ask participants to take out a clean sheet of paper and a pencil but not to write their names on it.

5.   Write the problem [point] on the flip chart so everyone can see it and then ask, "What are some ways we can deal with this in order to achieve the best possible outcome?"

6.   Ask each person to list up to ten ideas for achieving an optimal outcome.

7.   Collect the responses and give them to the facilitator, who will leave the room to study the replies and to prepare a synthesis of them.

8.   Continue with the training and when the facilitator returns, permit him or her, at the earliest possibly opening, to deliver the report.

FOLLOW-UP   Following the facilitator's report, if the topic and the suggestions for resolving it still appear too hot to handle, appoint a committee to take the report, leave the room, and return with a recommended course of action. The committee should include some of the most vocal position advocates.

Pass around a sheet of paper, with your name listed for the first entry and beside it, your recommendation for handling potentially disruptive topics. Continue to circulate the paper until you have one suggestion from each participant. If possible, type up the list and distribute it to participants before the end of the training session.

TRANSITION   *The greater your repertoire of skills for handling difficult people, difficult topics, and difficult situations, the more valuable you will be as an employee. I hope you will practice not only the Delphi Technique but a number of others that have been demonstrated today. Remember, you can say anything to anyone about anything. The reaction you get depends on how you say it.*

46

CLIPPING THE WINGS OF CREATIVITY

FORM

Teams of seven or eight participants discuss a pressing problem and brainstorm a list of ideas. They then decide on one item that can be eliminated and subject it to a final scrutiny. This energizer takes 10–15 minutes for completion.

FUNCTION

1. Divide the group into teams of seven or eight.

2. Begin with this background information:

More than sixty years ago, an American advertising executive, Alex Osborne, coined the term brainstorming to describe the cerebral explosions that occur when people are on a roll in their pursuit of ideas. Since then, the term has become part of our individual and collective creative consciousness.

There are guidelines associated with brainstorming:

All ideas are recorded.

Judgment is deferred.

People are expected to listen carefully to one another.

Only one person speaks at a time.

Ideas are piggybacked.

3. Ask each team to brainstorm a list of ten work-related or training-related problems.

4. Have each team select one problem and brainstorm possible solutions for about 5 minutes.

5. Next, ask the teams to decide which one solution should definitely be eliminated. Share this information with them as soon as each team has made its choice for elimination:

A survey by Lloyds Bank in England several years ago found that only twenty percent of paper clips were used to hold paper. The remainder were unwound and then used to clean fingernails, ears, and pipes. Others were twisted during phone conversations or at meetings as a means of relieving stress.

They were also found to be remarkably effective at reinforcing eyeglasses.

Although the originator of the humble paper clip never foresaw these additional uses, this study found that the majority of uses for paper clips were not associated with holding paper! By extension, there may be some value we have not yet considered in regard to this one item we are about to throw away.

6.   Having made their choice for elimination, teams will then subject the item to a final analysis by coming up with at least three benefits or advantages of the idea they are about to discard. Then, they will ask once more if it truly deserves to be eliminated. If so, it goes. If not, it remains on the list and the remaining ideas are scrutinized in the same way.

7.   Point out that such scrutiny should not be used in every brainstorming session. It works best when a short list of critical choices (such as those that evolve from strategic-planning sessions) has to be narrowed down even more. Because the short-list items are so valuable (they wouldn't have made it to the final cutting if they weren't), this process affords them one last chance to be considered.

FOLLOW-UP

Ask for business examples that demonstrate how initial rejection did not deter the originators of good ideas from pursuing them. As an illustration, use the example of the British general and prime minister, Arthur Wellington, whose own mother considered him a dunce. Yet, at age 46, he defeated Napoleon, who had been considered the world's greatest living general.

To illustrate the need to persevere despite the experts' opinions, use the story of Jockey Eddie Arcaro, who lost 250 straight races before winning one. He later held the world record for earning the most money as a jockey, in 1948, 1950, 1952, and 1955.

Finally, you can cite Beethoven (*Fidelio*), Puccini (*Madame Butterfly*), and Stravinsky (*The Rite of Spring*), all of whom had flops on opening night. Note that it was truly a hard day's night when the Beatles were turned down after auditioning for Decca Records. They were advised, "Guitar groups are on the way out."

TRANSITION

Certainly, we cannot subject every item tossed out through the list-reduction process to this kind of consideration. Nonetheless, this process does help prevent ideas or individuals from being railroaded; it does help prevent groupthink. For the remainder of this training session, I hope you will feel comfortable enough to argue for your points if you really feel strongly about them. Or, if we have had to cut short some discussion and you still wish to talk more about it, please see me at the break and we can explore it a bit further.

47

THE BIG 3

FORM

This energizer begins with a discussion of competencies related to the training topic. Those traits are then prioritized into a short list of three. The top three are next transferred to the lines within the circle on Handout 47-1, and participants rate themselves according to those standards. About 10 minutes will be needed, plus another 5 to obtain team averages.

FUNCTION

1. Lead a discussion of the core competencies associated with the topic of training. For example, in a class titled Introduction to Supervision, some prized knowledge, skills, and abilities could include the ability to lead, the willingness to empower, listening skills, technical expertise, et cetera. List 15 to 20 valued competencies.

2. Through a show of hands, reduce the list to the top three choices.

3. Distribute the handout and ask participants to rate themselves, on a scale of 1 to 100, reflecting the extent to which they feel they possess these abilities, skills, or knowledge.

4. Form teams of five to six participants and have them obtain average team scores for each of the three competencies.

5. Determine which team had the highest scores and crown them the team of experts. During the course of the subsequent training, as various issues and problems arise, turn the questions over to the team of experts first to learn their opinion or recommendations.

FOLLOW-UP

Have the team of experts break up and work with the remaining groups. Each group will then prepare a brief report, to be shared aloud with the others, in answer to this question: What specific steps can be taken (beyond training seminars) to increase our knowledge, skills, and abilities in these three areas?

Invite the head of Human Resources to hear these reports and to respond regarding the feasibility of the proposals.

TRANSITION

Socrates asserted that the unexamined life is not worth living. Add to that assertion the fact that time, for most of us, is an extremely precious commodity. If we are not periodically assess-

ing the direction in which we are moving, if we are not assessing what we have and what we need, then we are no doubt wasting the time of our lives. Further, we are probably not moving closer to our goals. Although this exercise is designed for application to training, it can also be used in a wide variety of situations.

Now, since we voted _____ [Insert one of the top three competencies] as an important attribute, let me explain how our next task will help you develop this particular skill....

HANDOUT 47-1

Directions: In the circle below, you will note three lines, each of which moves from 0 on the left to 100 on the right, with incremental notches along the way. Your first task is to write the top three competencies from the flip chart list onto these lines. Next, you will assess yourself, on a scale of 0 to 100: To what degree do you possess each competency? Indicate your self-assessment by placing an *X* above the number that corresponds to your assessment.

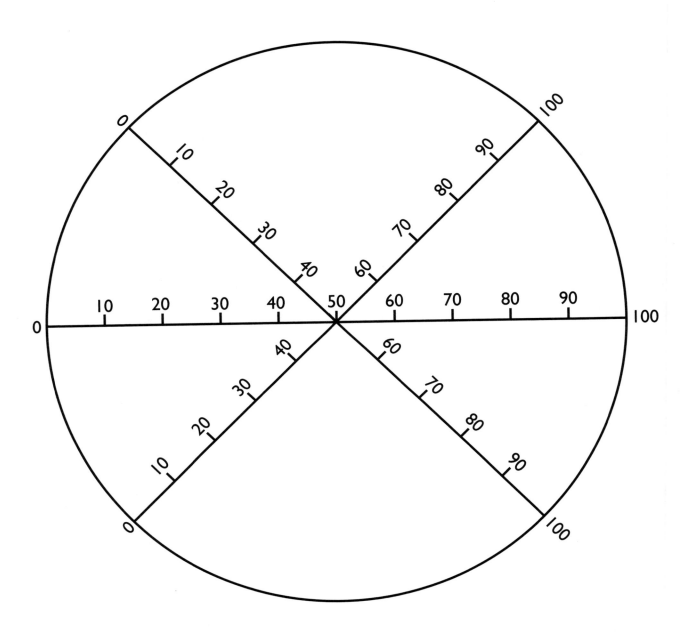

48

PANELS—WOODEN AND OTHERWISE

FORM

Using a hot topic that has arisen during a discussion of some aspect of the training, panel members will work to prepare their thoughts while the remaining participants meet with you to discuss ground rules. Plan on 30 minutes for full execution of this activity.

FUNCTION

1.   Begin with this mini-lecture:

The panel presentation is typically a lively exchange of ideas, opinions, and facts before an audience. The panel has a moderator, who controls both the flow of words and the time factor. (The moderator may also have to intervene if the panel members get off the topic or if they demonstrate less-than-professional conduct.) The most interesting panels include people with differing points of view and sufficient knowledge to speak with authority—people, in other words, who do not appear stiff or wooden.

Typically, we find panels at professional conferences or seminars. We also find panel members invited to address meetings of intraorganizational groups. By attending such a meeting, you will have an opportunity to watch and learn from the members as they handle questions from the audience members on the spot. By organizing such a meeting, you will have an opportunity to demonstrate your leadership. And by serving on the panel itself, you will have an opportunity to develop your own communication skills.

Today, you will have an opportunity to organize or serve on a panel. We are going to explore the differing viewpoints on this topic: _____. [Use one that has been tossed around during the training session, or use one of these about training in general: Should employees pay for the training they receive if, after three months, it is determined they have not put it to use? Should employes contribute to the cost of their training? Should there be final exams at the end of training programs? Should employees, in whom training investments have been made, be required to remain with their company for at least a year following the training?]

2.   Ask for volunteers who have strong views on the issue. Select equal numbers of volunteers to serve on the pro and on the con sides (at least three people on each side).

3.   As the sides meet (for about 15 minutes) to plan their verbal strategies, you will meet with the remaining members of the class. Ask for a volunteer to serve as moderator. Then establish ground rules, including time constraints, that the moderator will be expected to enforce. Before the panelists begin, the moderator will inform them of the ground rules.

Advise the nonpanel class participants they are expected to prepare a written critique of the presentation as they are watching it. Of special importance is their assessment of how well the moderator maintained control. They should also make note of especially effective comebacks from the panel members. (Note: If time remains, informally discuss with participants some of the panel presentations they have seen on television.)

4.   Hold the actual panel presentation, allowing time at the end for input and questions from the audience.

FOLLOW-UP

Invite panel members from senior management, from various departments, or even from outside agencies to discuss a given issue, such as workplace safety. If the training lasts longer than a day, assign the watching of a panel television program, such as *Crossfire* or *Rivera Live*. Have participants report the next day on elements of the program they felt were especially effective.

Encourage the formation of a panel to address the relevance of the training received with prospective enrollees.

TRANSITION

Career strategists insist that those individuals interested in moving ahead in their chosen professions need to learn how to stand out from the crowd. If you have such an ambition—and most of us do—organizing a panel presentation is an excellent means of gaining professional visibility. You may choose to assemble or serve on an informal panel. Or, you may choose to really make a grand gesture by organizing a conference or symposium for _____ [Mention the training topic and the kind of people who would be likely to attend a conference on this topic]. *The panel presentation could be one of the special presentations at the meeting.*

Whether or not you work again with panels, however, you will work again with the topic our panel examined. In fact, the next thing we are going to do involves _____ [Relate the next element of the course outline to the topic the panel just discussed].

49

THE DASHING YOUNG PLAN ON THE FLYING TRAPEZE

FORM

Based on a Stephen Covey quote, this energizer asks participants, working in small groups of four or five, to formulate a plan to most effectively employ the training they are receiving. The exercise requires no advance preparation other than duplicating the worksheet, and it takes about 15 minutes.

FUNCTION

1. Share this quotation by Stephen Covey with the whole group: "I look at an organization as a high-wire trapeze act, and today there's no net." Repeat it, slowly and loudly, and then say, "Let's think about that for a minute." Lead a short discussion, inviting interpretations of what Covey may have meant by his comment.

2. Divide the class into teams of four or five.

3. Distribute Handout 49-1.

4. Allow about 10 minutes for completing the worksheets.

5. Ask each team to share their insights.

FOLLOW-UP

Suggest the that teams further explore their ideas by writing an article, to be actually submitted to training publications or perhaps even to Covey's *Executive Excellence* magazine.

Ask for a volunteer to synthesize the team reports into a summary to be shared with the supervisors of attendees. Encourage employees, once their supervisors have received this report, to discuss implementation of these plans.

TRANSITION

Opinions about the value of planning range from the elegant (Peter Drucker: "Long-range planning does not deal with future decisions, but with the future of present decisions.") to the entertaining (Yogi Berra: "If you don't know where you're going, you could wind up someplace else."). One thing is certain, though: Without deliberate thought regarding what to do with what you've got, you cannot optimize the value of what you have. Let these plans you've formulated serve as a backdrop for the remainder of our training session. Plug ideas into the outline you've already created. For example, we are going to learn next about _____, [Mention the next concept to be presented]. Where would this fit into your plan?

HANDOUT 49-1

Directions: Working with three or four others, answer the following questions based on Mr. Covey's observation ("I look at an organization as a high-wire trapeze act, and today there's no net"). Then, use your answers to formulate a plan for maximizing the organization's investment in you specifically and in training generally.

1. How or why could your organization be described as a "hire-wire trapeze act"?
    _____
    _____

2. How could training be used as a "net"?_____
    _____
    _____

3. If you were to assume ringmaster leadership, what could you actually do to offer some security to those taking "mid-air" risks?_____
    _____
    _____

4. What "leaps" of faith will you, as an attendee of today's training, have to make in order to most fully use the training you have been given?_____
    _____
    _____

5. If your life depended on demonstrating skills (or knowledge) you have acquired thus far in this training program, what could you demonstrate?_____
    _____
    _____

6. What, specifically, would make you feel safe as you build upon the knowledge you are acquiring here today?_____
    _____
    _____

7. What other "artists" might be willing to join you on the training trapeze? (What alliances could you form in order to implement or extend this training)?_____
    _____
    _____

8. What might cause you to lose your concentration and thus jeopardize your best intentions regarding the training you are receiving? How could you then recapture that concentration?
    _____
    _____

Review what's been written here and discussed with your team. Then, formulate a four-step plan (in sequential order) telling exactly, specifically, how you can best make use of this training once you have returned to work.

50

SNURFING USA

FORM

In about 10 minutes, small groups of four or five will be able to come up with a new term related to events occurring in their organization, field, or industry. These words can serve as starting points for subsequent courses of action.

FUNCTION

1. Share this mini-lecture with the class as a whole:

A neologism is simply a newly coined word. For example, when Pat Riley, former coach of the Los Angeles Lakers, hoped his team would win three championships in a row, he coined the word three-peat. *(The Lakers never did claim that honor but the Chicago Bulls did in subsequent years. Pat Riley, who had legally copyrighted the term, earned a great deal of money from it.)*

To explain the impact of electronics upon aviation, the word avionics *was coined. To describe the tunnel that goes beneath the English Channel, the word* chunnel *was created. To describe political campaigns that contain negative information, the word* slampaign *was designed. Sometimes the new word captures a novel, creative concept (*televangelism*). At other times, the new word expresses an objective (*three-peat*) or suggests a solution.*

The most popular neologism of all may be the one associated with a relatively new sport. It was created in 1965, when Sherman Poppen walked outside his Michigan home on a wintry day and stared at a hill covered with snow. The wind blew the snow into rippling patterns that reminded Mr. Poppen of a wave. This inventor, whose fascination with surfing was stifled by the climatic realities of his resident state, thought about riding the crests of waves.

Within hours, he had created a surfboard for the snow. His wife created the words to go with it: snurfers *are snow-surfers and* snurfing *is what they do. They also created a huge market for the invention. Millions have been converted to the new sport since the neighborhood children in Muskegon, Michigan first enjoyed Mr. Poppen's snow-inspired invention.*

2.   Ask participants to work in small groups and to list ten current events, problems, or relevant terms from any five different worlds: the worlds of business, politics, geography, crafts, medicine, sports, education, music, et cetera (yielding a list of about 50 items).

3.   Next ask them to create at least one new word that speaks to a future state of affairs or even to training that might be required. For example, in a class for office professionals, the word *cybertary* was suggested as a replacement for the current term, *secretary.* The new word alludes to the frequency with which today's secretary is expected to travel in cyberspace. Along with this allusion is the implication that if today's secretaries have not received extensive training in computer skills, they had best acquire such if they hope to remain competitive in terms of career opportunities.

4.   Finally, have teams explore the possibilities for new products, new services, or even new policies that might result from their neologisms.

5.   Ask a spokesperson from each team to share the new word, along with its implications for next steps to be taken.

FOLLOW-UP

Distribute old newspapers to class members and ask them to find examples of neologisms. (Technocrats in the class will no doubt be able to provide a *plethabulary* (*plethora* + *vocabulary*) of new words spawned by the electronic revolution.)

Assign the creation of a new word specifically related to the transference of skills or knowledge from the training room to the workplace. Select the best of the creations and use it as widely as you can in the organization as a means of emphasizing the value of training.

TRANSITION

*Let me share with you a neologism I've created—*cognisieve.* The cognisieve is a filter or strainer or sieve that permits you to remove extraneous knowledge and let only the most salient information get through. For example, in the first two sentences I've just spoken, there were thirty-five words. If your cognisieve is working, you can reduce those thirty-five words to a mere handful and still retain the essential message. Anyone want to try?* [Elicit responses, such as, "Filter out unimportant details"]

As we continue with the course, there will be an overload of words and ideas and images coming your mental way, especially in this next segment. Don't try to remember or write down every single word. Instead, try to capture the cogent points and fit them into your mental outlines. Periodically, I'll stop and call on someone to share the cognisieve'd *concepts.*

51

SELF-SYMBOLS

FORM

Participants will work for a few minutes to describe how they feel about the knowledge they have thus far acquired and will then share their self-symbols with others. This energizer takes 5–10 minutes to conduct and requires no material other than paper and pencils for participants. (You might have a dictionary at each table in case someone on the team is stuck.)

FUNCTION

1. Ask each person to make a list of 25 random nouns—any 25 that come to mind (e.g., sponge, pool, umbrella, leaf, clock, etc.)

2. Divide the group into teams of four or five, asking them to quickly share their lists of nouns as a means of stimulating thought.

3. Each person will then select one word (from the lists, from the dictionary, or from their own heads) and will use that noun to explain how they feel about the training they have received thus far. For example, some might feel like a sponge, absorbing knowledge, soaking up the spills created by excited, animated discussions, bending their minds into new shapes, and so on.

4. Have the teams select an especially relevant description and share it with the class as a whole.

FOLLOW-UP

Have participants write their descriptions, anonymously, in one-paragraph essays. At break time, collect them and quickly sort them into two piles: those that are positive (like the sponge) and those that are not. (For example, "I feel like I'm drowning in a pool of knowledge" would be placed in the negative pile.) After the break, lead a discussion about how the negative reactions could be converted into more positive reactions.

Share the descriptions with the editor of the organizational newspaper, issue by issue, to gain a wider audience for these perspectives on training.

TRANSITION

[Choose one of the descriptions offered by participants and make a transition such as this. Or, revert back to the image of the sponge.]

There is just one difference between the actual sponge and the human sponge—the natural sponge always returns to its origi-

nal form. You, by contrast, are expected to walk out of here a different person than you were when you walked in. In other words, if you are thinking the very same thoughts when you leave that you were thinking when you entered, if nothing new penetrated your gray matter, then I will have failed in my instructional obligation and you will have wasted considerable personal time and corporate money.

Yes, continue soaking up as much as you can. But don't stop there. Let your new knowledge inspire you to do something differently, to effect positive change. To do otherwise is to lose an opportunity.

52

RUNNING THE COURSE

FORM

Working in groups of six or seven, participants will first make a list of at least 20 things they remember learning up to this point in the training session. (This activity is best conducted near the end of the day when participants have been exposed to enough information for them to establish a logical flow for it.) They will then organize those items into four or five categories, one category per sheet of paper. Next, they will post their categories at four or five stations around the room and invite others to walk around and see the various ways different groups clustered the knowledge points. Have clean sheets of paper (at least five) and marking pens available for each group. This energizer takes at least 15 minutes to complete.

FUNCTION

1. Divide the group into teams of six or seven if the group is a large one. Otherwise, form teams of four participants. Have each team select a name for itself.

2. Ask the teams to brainstorm a list of at least 20 things that stand out in their minds in reference to the training they have received thus far.

3. Next, have them divide the items into four or five logical categories. They will transfer the categories onto clean sheets of 8 $\frac{1}{2}$ x 11-inch paper, one sheet per category. Each sheet will have the team's name at the top.

4. The teams will now discuss the order in which those categories would ideally be presented. They will indicate this sequence by writing 1 for the category they feel should be presented first, 2 for the category that should come second, and so on.

5. Finally, the teams will post their numbered sheets around the room.

6. Have the teams circulate around the room to see what the others have done and to make notes on the ordering and the items within each category, both where they agree and where they disagree.

7. Call on a spokesperson from each team to tell his or her team's thinking about how the other teams decided to "run the course."

FOLLOW-UP

Ask the teams to quickly list the steps to be followed in the process of changing a flat tire. In theory, the same steps should appear in the same order, no matter which team is writing them. In all likelihood, though, there will be little similarity. Lead from this experiment to the importance of analyzing work processes.

Encourage participants to join (or form) teams when they return to work so standard operating procedures (or flow diagrams at the very least) can be written for the most important work processes.

TRANSITION

There are, of course, any number of ways in which the same information could be organized. The ideas you have shared today will certainly be considered as I make preparations to teach the next version of this training program. The important thing, though, is that you are actually engaging with the knowledge that has been presented. You are thinking about it, questioning it, discussing it, organizing it. The more you physically interact with knowledge, the greater will be your possession of it. Confucius wasn't kidding when he said, "I hear and I forget. I see and I remember. I do and I learn." Continue this kind of interaction with knowledge, especially if the information is altogether new or extremely complex. In fact, you are about to receive a complex challenge. The next topic on our instructional agenda is _____ [Supply the term, formula, or theory you are about to present].

53

FROM UNKNOWING TO UNKNOWINGLY

FORM

This energizer begins with a presentation of the four stages of learning and a brief discussion of each. (Have Post-It notes available.) Divided into teams of four, participants then share their assessments of the stages they find themselve. nt. You will need 15–20 minutes for completion but no special equipment or materials other than the Post-It notes.

FUNCTION

1.   At the top of a flip chart page, write the words Most Critical Knowledge and Skills. Lead a brief discussion to identify some of the most important things participants, their supervisors, their teams, their coworkers, and the organization itself expects they will learn in this training. (Five to ten entries is a sufficient number.) Post the flip chart sheet where everyone can see it.

2.   Write these four combinations on the top of flip chart sheets, one combination per sheet, and post the four sheets around the room.

1) Unknowing—Unskilled

2) Knowing—Unskilled

3) Knowing—Skilled

4) Unknowingly—Skilled

Explain that these are commonly regarded as the four stages of learning.

3.   Divide the class into teams of four and distribute a small stack of Post-It notes (3 x 5-inch is an ideal size) to each team.

4.   Ask the teams to discuss what they believe occurs at each stage and to record their thoughts on the Post-It notes. As soon as they have finished the first interpretation (Unknowing—Unskilled), they are to post their responses on the sheet that has these words at the top. Then they will work on the next combination (Knowing—Unskilled), and so on until all four combinations have been considered.

5.   When each team has finished defining the four steps, quickly review the meanings. (The combinations are really self-explanatory, except the last. *Unknowingly* refers to skills performed at such a high level of proficiency that the performer works unthinkingly, automatically.) You

could use the example of learning to drive a car to trace the progression through the various stages.

6.   Now return to the flip chart with the list of five to ten critical competencies. Ask each team to discuss among themselves the stages that various team members find themselves at in relation to the listed skills.

FOLLOW-UP

Use the critical competencies as a means of evaluating the effectiveness of the training. In lieu of the typical evaluation form, have participants list the stages they find themselves at for each of these skills.

Divide the class into two large groups. Have the first discuss ways to move from the second stage to the third. Ask the second group to list ways to move from the third stage to the fourth. Then suggest that participants establish a buddy system whereby they can help one another reach the stage of skill development at which the skill is practiced as a habit.

TRANSITION

I suspect everyone here—except me, of course—will be at the Unknowing—Unskilled stage as far as _____ [Supply the name of the next technique or theory you intend to present] *is concerned. Let me share it with you now, so that you can at least move to the stage of Knowing about it, even though you won't have a chance to develop the actual skill until after* [Supply appropriate time reference].

54

THERE ARE FEWER RULES THAN YOU THINK

FORM

Although participants will think this energizer is a test of their ability to improve a process, it is really a test of their ability to break free from self-imposed assumptions. The exercise takes about 5 minutes including debriefing. All you will need for it is a lightweight ball, no smaller than a tennis ball and no larger than a beach ball.

FUNCTION

1.   Ask for nine volunteers to come to the front of the room and form a circle. (Stand three feet away from the people on either side of you and casually arrange for the same distance to be kept among the others.)

2.   Appoint a timekeeper who will time how long it takes for the tossed ball to be returned to the original thrower (you, in this case).

3.   Ask the remaining participants to serve as observers, who will make notes about the process of improving a process.

4.   Explain to the volunteers that their task is to improve the process of getting the ball from the original thrower all the way around the circle and back to the original thrower. The only stipulation is that the ball must be handled by each person in the same order reflected in the original tossing.

5.   Alert the timekeeper to begin and throw the ball to someone in the circle. He or she throws it to someone else. The process continues until the last person tosses the ball back to you.

6.   At that point, ask the timekeeper how much time elapsed.

7.   Now ask the participants in the circle if they could go through the process again and shave a few seconds off their time.

8.   After several time-shaving tries, someone usually realizes that if they move in closer to one another, they can save considerable time. Have them try it and see.

9.   Occasionally, someone will realize that they don't have to toss the ball at all. They can simple move as close to one another as possible and then merely place their hands upon the ball in the correct sequence and still fulfill the requirements of the process.

10. Debrief by allowing time for the observers to share the notes they took as the volunteers were working to improve the process.

FOLLOW-UP

At several points during the remaining hours of training, ask, "Is there a better way to do this?"—whether you are discussing an industry practice, an organizational policy, or simply a classroom procedure.

Write the name of a product or service provided by the organization that employs some or all of the participants. Then give groups of four or five a 5-minute period to list all the ways that product or service can be improved. Typically, numerous feasible ideas are produced, many of which can be quickly and inexpensively implemented.

TRANSITION

Tom Peters is known for many wise and witty pronouncements. One of my favorites is this: "If you have gone a whole week without being disobedient, you are doing yourself and your organization a disservice." By disobedient, of course, he does not mean breaking the rules for the sake of breaking the rules. Instead, question the way things are done so that continuous improvement can occur.

True leaders and true authority figures do not mind being questioned. Already today, there have been several instances when one of you has questioned something I have said. I don't mind that at all. In fact, I think it's healthy to regard learning as a give-and-take situation. We saw in the ball tossing that several of you had ideas for improving upon the original process I had established.

For the remainder of the program, please, continue to ask me questions. I am sincerely interested in improving the process of learning. What could we do better than it is being done or better than the way I outlined? By all means, if there is something you disagree with, let us hear your voice.

This next theory [concept, principle—whatever you plan to present next] is one with which you may initially disagree. But please, hear me out. You many wind up concurring with its basic premise. If not, though, please offer your opinion. We'll all be the richer for it.

55

MASTER FILES

This energizer is an ongoing one, requiring participants to place a 3 x 5-inch card (with their names and the concepts or skills they feel they have mastered on it) into a file folder as soon as they feel they thoroughly understand one of the focal points of the instructional program. At any given point during the training day, you will call a halt to the regular training, ask the table groups to count the number of cards in their folders, and award a token prize (5 extra minutes at lunchtime, for example) to the team with the most cards.

To heighten the sense of competition, you can pull a card and ask the person who wrote it to demonstrate his or her understanding of the concept. The actual exercise takes only a few minutes (although the process of adding cards to the folder is a continuous one). You will need ten 3 x 5-inch cards per participant and one folder for each table.

To ensure fairness, have the same number of people at each table; four is ideal. If this is not possible, ask the one, two, or three left-over participants not to engage in the skill-on-a-card process.

FUNCTION

1.   Distribute a file folder (labeled Master File in big letters) to each team of participants, along with ten 3 x 5-inch cards for each participant. (Note: If you put masking tape along the sides of the folder, it will prevent the cards from slipping out.)

2.   Ask participants to write their names at the tops of their cards.

3.   Explain that for the remainder of the training day, you would like them to write on the cards any chunk of knowledge or any skill over which they feel they have acquired mastery. They are to continue adding cards to the team folder as the day progresses.

4.   Periodically (but not always) after presenting an instructional segment, encourage those participants who feel they have complete mastery of the idea or skill to note it on a 3 x 5-inch card, along with their names, and place the card in the folder.

5.   From time to time, stop the training flow and ask the teams to count the number of cards in the folders.

6.   Give some sort of bonus to the team with the most cards.

FOLLOW-UP

The true test of learning is being able to answer Yes to this question: "Could you perform this skill (or demonstrate mastery of this knowledge) if your life depended on it?" As part of the periodic review process, list all of the major points or course objectives on the flip chart. For each, find one person who can answer Yes to that question. Have him or her demonstrate mastery of the skill or knowledge.

Encourage a friendly rivalry by promising to write a glowing letter to the supervisor (and the supervisor's manager) of the person who had the largest number of mastery cards in the folder. Keep your promise.

Ask for examples and interpretations of Patrick White's comment, "I forget what I was taught. I only remember what I've learnt."

TRANSITION

Although we have kept a competition going here with mastery, know that you are truly only competing with yourself. As athletes do with physical skills, you should be trying to acquire as much knowledge as you possibly can. The best investment, actually, is not in stocks or bonds. The best investment you can ever make is in yourself. And when you leave knowing more than you did when you came in, you can call yourself a winner indeed.

56

ALWAYS SAY "NEVER"

FORM

Divide the class into two large groups. Allot only 5 minutes for the two teams, using flip charts and marking pens, to record their respective lists (as long a list as possible) of sentences beginning with Always or Never in relation to the training. Then take another 5 minutes to review the lists (subtracting or supplementing as needed).

FUNCTION

1.   Divide the class into two large groups: the Always and the Nevers. Give each group marking pens and flip chart paper.

2.   Ask them to think back on all they have heard and seen and thought about thus far and to formulate some Always and Never statements. For example, in a business writing class, you might use the following:

Always put quotations marks after the period.
Never use the apostrophe with possessive pronouns.

3.   Allow 5 minutes for the lists to be compiled.

4.   When the time is up, determine which team had the longer list and award them the kudos they deserve.

FOLLOW-UP

Keep your own list of Sometimes statements and use it as a review mechanism near the end of the training program.

Find pertinent quotations that begin with Always, Never, or Sometimes. Use them as the basis of a discussion. Here are a few that might be useful:

Always suspect everybody. (Charles Dickens)
Always do right. This will gratify some people and astonish the rest. (Mark Twain)
Never give up. (Winston Churchill)
Never do today what you can put off till tomorrow. (William Rands)
Never be mean in anything; never be false; never be cruel. (Charles Dickens)

TRANSITION

It's not often that we encounter absolutes in life, especially not with technology, which changes so very rapidly. But there are certain basics as far as some knowledge is concerned—some truths that will remain constant no matter who the learner, who the trainer, what the year. We have encountered some of those absolutes by way of this activity.

Here's another absolute for you... [Present a fundamental truth next, one that reflects a core value or basic principle of the training you are providing].

57

EXHILARATING DISRUPTIONS

FORM

This energizer, which calls for some creativity on your part, works especially well when the class is bogged down by a too-serious or heated discussion; when they have expended considerable mental energy working through a particularly challenging segment of the program; or when they begin to nod off after a too-heavy lunch. It requires the appointment of two observers early in the day. They will, upon a prearranged signal from you, record the atmosphere or the mood of the class at a low point, such as those already mentioned.

Once they have begun making their notes, you will create an exhilarating disruption, lasting only a few minutes. The observers will make note of the mood immediately following the disruption. Then, they will share their pre- and postintervention descriptions with the class before you all return to the business at hand.

FUNCTION

1. Ask two of the more insightful, verbal participants to serve as observers. Explain what they are to do (as described in the Form section).

2. Give the signal to the observers. Then, engage in something that will cause some creative tension in the training room. Some suggestions follow:

Prearrange to have an outsider enter the room and smash a cream pie in your face as you are lecturing.

Put on roller blades and skate around the room.

Play some rock 'n' roll music and dance for a few minutes.

Slip the mask of a famous person on your face and begin talking in his or her persona.

Begin juggling balls in the air.

Sing in a falsetto voice.

Release a small animal (kitten, frog, gerbil) into the classroom.

Pass out one-dollar bills.

Take out a bottle with a famous alcoholic label but one that you have filled with water, excuse yourself by saying you cannot wait any longer, and guzzle it down. (Be sure to show them afterward that it was indeed only water.)

Use a child's bottle of bubble-soap and start to blow bubbles.

Take out some pizza dough you've kept hidden and start to toss it in the air. After 12 tosses, let it land on your head.

3.   Upon completion of your performance, ask the observers to report what they noted.

4.   Explain that appropriate and brief disruptions in the normal routine of work patterns can actually energize employees, just as this disruption energized the group here and now.

FOLLOW-UP

A variation on the exhilarating disruption theme has you lecturing when suddenly the door opens and someone (preferably a stranger to the group) walks in and begins to unplug the overhead projector. You politely explain that you need it and that you had arranged to have it. The other person expresses insincere regrets but continues to remove it. The situation escalates into an altercation, with the other person much angrier than you. He or she finally storms out of the room, without the projector, makes several nasty and loud comments, and slams the door.

Express your surprise and dismay to the group and explain that you want to report this person to administration but that you want verification from eye witnesses. Have them write short accounts of what happened. Collect them and then explain the situation was set up. Now use the written accounts as a teaching tool: Despite the fact that everyone saw and heard the same thing, their versions of what occurred will probably vary widely.

Suggest that a volunteer committee be formed to plan appropriate and brief disruptions at work, once a week but not always on the same day.

TRANSITION

Although I heard some of you giggling as the pie met my eyes [Substitute the appropriate words for the actual disruption], there is a serious point I want to make here. As dedicated as you are to learning here in this room and as dedicated as you are to working back in the workplace, the truth is that we all need to break away from time to time from the tedium of intense concentration.

This is probably why there are teams like the Joy Club at Ben & Jerry's Ice Cream Factory. These teams find unusual, but suitable, ways to make work more enjoyable. For me, knowledge is its own reward. But I know not everyone feels quite the same way. I promise you, though, you will find our next task almost as much fun as watching someone throw a pie in my face [Make reference to the actual event that occurred]. (Note: Be sure to use this energizer right after a draining experience and right before an easy one.)

58

ALLITERATIVE ASSOCIATIONS

FORM

You can use this energizer at various points during the course of the day as a means of reflecting on what has been covered to this point. Simply allocate 5 minutes for participants (working in triads) to list as many words as they can, starting with a certain letter of the alphabet, related to the topic of the training program. Take a few additional minutes to determine the winning triad. (Note: Three cans of alphabet soup make ideal token prizes.)

FUNCTION

1. Divide the group into triads.

2. Write a large P on a flip chart.

3. Advise the triads they will have only 5 minutes to produce as long a list as possible of words relevant to the training topic that begin with the letter P.

4. After 5 minutes, call time. Determine which triad had the longest list.

5. Before awarding their prizes, ask them to read their list. Challenge them to explain any words whose relevancy is not immediately clear.

FOLLOW-UP

Periodically, take another letter of the alphabet and energize participants by having them write other words, beginning with that letter, related to the training that has occurred *since* the last exercise.

Take a word with pivotal significance to the training topic and ask teams to write a related word for each of the letters in the word. The related words have to start with the letter being used. For example, in a training program for telemarketers, *call center* is an important term. The task could produce results like these:

c	=	customer
a	=	attitude
l	=	language
l	=	listening
c	=	challenge
e	=	energy

n	=	numbers
t	=	time
e	=	education
r	=	return

TRANSITION

To be sure, you deserve an E for both Effort and Excellence in your Endeavor to complete this Energizer. You're going to need a lot of Energy for the next one, which will require you to... [Briefly explain the nature of the next assignment].

59

(COURT) CASE STUDY

FORM

Participants spend a few moments, working in groups of four of five, deciding the outcome of a court case. Then, using the legal ruling as a basis for discussion, they will engage in a discussion focusing on obvious points that may have been made and those not made in relation to the training topic. Duplicate the case study and allow 10 minutes for this exercise.

FUNCTION

1.   Explain that litigation frequency and costs are quite high: One in five managers will be involved in litigation at some point in his or her career. Even if the the individual or the company wins the case, there are still attorney fees to pay. It's best to avoid even the suggestion of illegal or improper behavior. Tell participants they will have a chance today to determine, in a case study, if behavior was illegal or improper.

2.   Ask participants to form groups of 3, 5, or 7 participants. (Because they will need a majority-rules vote on the case, have uneven numbers in the team.)

3.   Distribute Handout 59-1.

4.   Allow about 5 minutes for the teams to decide how they would rule on the case.

5.   Call on the teams to share their answers, then reveal the actual ruling:

The courts granted a judgment to the company and so the case never even made it to trial. It is true that the Americans with Disabilities Act (ADA) forces employers to inform employees about the accommodations available to them. However, the court ruled in this case that the employee already knew about those accommodations because he had already used them. In its actual ruling, the court said there was no need to "reiterate self-evident options."

6.   Emphasize the need to stress the obvious—particularly where legal or safety issues may be concerned (despite the court's ruling on self-evident reiterations).

7.   Draw parallels to the assumptions you, as trainer or facilitator, have made about the course, its relevance, and the participants taking

the course. Tell what you thought was perfectly obvious and ask if those points have been equally obvious to participants. Ask what *they* thought was perfectly obvious and then discuss how obvious it was to you. Continue to discuss what may seem obvious to the supervisors and coworkers with whom they work, if only as far as the training itself is concerned.

FOLLOW-UP

Collect newspaper stories of business-related court cases. Use them as discussion starters on various aspects of the training topic you are presenting.

Invite an employment law expert (perhaps from the Human Resources department) to address the group concerning relevant legislation that could have an impact on the way they work.

TRANSITION

It doesn't take a Philadelphia lawyer to figure out that we have an obligation—moral, if not legal—to take full advantage of the training offered here. The case study we've examined and the discussion we've had about it both point to the fact that we often assume things are "perfectly obvious" when they may not be so obvious to others. I hope it is obvious to all of you that you are expected to use this training, to do something with it. Before the session is over, I'm going to ask each of you to tell me one thing you will do to apply the knowledge and skills you have acquired here today. [Remember to ask each person, near the end of the training session, exactly how he or she will utilize the training]

Directions: The federal government has enacted legislation that protects employees in general and select groups of employees in particular. One of those groups is Americans with disabilities. Whether or not you are familiar with the intricacies of the Americans with Disabilities Act (ADA), think about the ruling you would have made if you were the judge in this real-life case (the names of individuals involved have been changed).

Pat Swiantek was the supervisor of a large department at Acme Manufacturing. He was conducting an informal performance review with Terry Wiles, one of his marginal performers. "You just are not putting out the work that others do," he told him. "I'm sorry about this but I will have to let you go."

Terry quickly pointed out, "Pat, you are aware of my disability. There's no way I can get my work done when I'm suffering from those migraines."

Pat felt this was an excuse, and pointed out that there were a number of accommodations for employees like Terry.

"I don't know what 'accommodations' you're talking about," Terry countered immediately.

Pat maintained his composure. Lowering his voice, he pointed out, "Terry, you know we have a medical center. You can go there when you're not well and that way, you wouldn't have to worry about the quality of your work bogging down. And, of course, you can always take a sick day—then you can't be penalized for not keeping the production levels up."

"That's what you mean by 'accommodation'?" Terry sounded incredulous. "I know the law," he asserted, "and the law says you have to tell me about available accommodations."

"What do you mean, we have to tell you?" Pat replied. "You've been to the medical center. You know you can take sick days. It's obvious that we have a medical center and sick days for people who are not well."

"It's not obvious to me," Terry shouted. "You violated the ADA law. And...the next time you see me, it'll be in court."

As a team, decide if you would have ruled in favor of Terry or in favor of Acme.

60

IT'S IN THE CARDS

FORM

After listening to a brief lecture on intuitive intelligence, participants will have an opportunity to determine if they have this intellectual power. They will work in triads during this exercise, which takes about 10 minutes. You will have to make copies of the handout cards (one set for each triad) and of the Observer's Form (one for each triad). (Note: If possible, glue cardboard to the backs of the cards after you have cut them and laminate or put wide transparent tape over them. Doing so will enable you to use them repeatedly. It will also prevent the testee from seeing what the cards have written on them.)

FUNCTION

1.   Present this mini-lecture. (Note: Use your own examples, if possible, related to the actual course you are presenting.)

Trainers like myself know there is something called intuitive intelligence that some learners have. Somehow, even though they have not been exposed to a particular theory or the work of a particular expert, they have an intuitive feel for the essence of the research that has been done.

Here is an example of what I mean. Sometimes, I draw a continuum on the flip chart like this. [Proceed to replicate this continuum on the flip chart.]

autocratic   democratic   laissez-faire

I next ask for a volunteer to come up and place an X to show where his or her management style falls along this continuum. [If one of the participants is in a supervisory position, ask him or her to do this.]

And, ordinarily, someone places an X somewhere along this line as we have just seen _____ [Supply volunteer's name] do right now.

Once in a very rare while, however, I find a participant who refuses to do this, someone who says, "I can't really place an

X on this line because I don't have a style as such. The way I operate depends on a number of things—the situation, the nature of the work to be done, the nature of the people I am supervising."

I then ask if this person has ever heard of the work of Professor Fred Fiedler of the University of Illinois or of his Contingency Theory of management. If the person has not, then he or she has actually displayed intuitive intelligence, for the response he or she gave is exactly what the Contingency Theory is all about.

2.   Form triads now. (Note: If one or two people are left over, assign them to other triads.) Ask each person to tell his or her partners if he or she believes he or she has intuitive intelligence.

3.   Explain that participants will have a chance to find out if they indeed have this special power. Ask two people in the triad to be the testers and the third person to be the testee. The testers will sit facing the testee, so the cards cannot be seen by the testee.

4.   Explain that the cards could have a single geometric shape (hold up an example) or a few shapes combined (hold up a multiple-shape example).

5.   Give the cards to one tester and the Observer's Form to the second tester. They will then test the third person by asking, "What is the geometric shape or shapes I am holding in my hand right now?" The second tester will note if the testee selected the right answer and will record it on the Observer's Form. The same question will be asked for each of the 18 cards.

6.   The cards should be shuffled and then handed face down to the new tester (who was just the testee). The former observer now takes the part of the testee and the tester who asked the question now has a chance to serve as the observer. He or she uses the same Observer's Form and the second round begins.

7.   After everyone has had a chance to participate in all three roles, ask each triad who was the most intuitive person on their team. Then compare the teams' top scorers to learn who, in the entire class, seems to be the most intuitive person of all.

FOLLOW-UP   Ask for a show of hands to learn how many people regard themselves as intuitive problem solvers: They don't analyze problems or seek the most logical solutions but, instead, do what *feels* like the right solution. Then ask how many of the intuitive problem solvers have actually tracked results to learn if this is indeed an effective way of solving problems. Suggest that they form posttraining teams to assist one another in enhancing their problem-solving skills.

Lead a short discussion, using these questions as prompts:

What was the worst intuitive solution or decision you made recently?

What led you to make such a decision in the first place?

Who do you know who invariably seems to make excellent intuitive decisions?

What have you learned about or from such a person?

Can you think of some examples of intuitive intelligence that you yourself have had—occasions when you realized that you knew something or thought about something in exactly the same way the experts think about it?

Are you more logical or creative? How many of you feel you are lateralized, or as logical as you are creative?

What is your problem-solving or decision-making style?

TRANSITION

The next thing we are going to study is _____ [Supply the next concept you intend to present]. *Who among you feels he or she has some intuitive intelligence concerning this concept?* [As participants respond, record their ideas on the flip chart, along with their names. Then, after the lecture, return to their comments to see how many did indeed display an intuitive knowledge.]

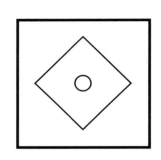 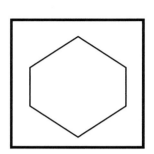

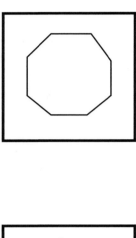  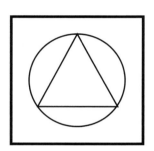

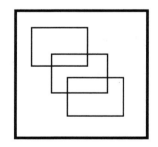 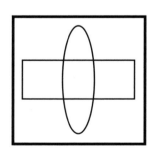 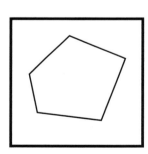

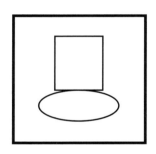

HANDOUT 60-2

Directions: Sit beside the tester who has the cards with geometric shapes on them. As the testee is being asked what geometric shape or shapes the tester is holding, you will write either Right or Wrong for each of the eighteen cards. (Pass this to a second observer when the experiment is concluded.)

1_____   2_____   3_____
4_____   5_____   6_____
7_____   8_____   9_____
10_____   11_____   12_____
13_____   14_____   15_____
16_____   17_____   18_____

You are the observer for the second round. Follow the instructions above. (Pass this form to the third observer upon completion of the second test.)

1_____   2_____   3_____
4_____   5_____   6_____
7_____   8_____   9_____
10_____   11_____   12_____
13_____   14_____   15_____
16_____   17_____   18_____

Now, the third person will be tested and you will be the observer as the testing is done. Note here whether the answers given were Right or Wrong.

1_____   2_____   3_____
4_____   5_____   6_____
7_____   8_____   9_____
10_____   11_____   12_____
13_____   14_____   15_____
16_____   17_____   18_____

61

HOW'M I DOIN'?

FORM

This energizer should be used at about the halfway point in the course, for it has participants tell you how you are doing via forms that ask what should be continued in terms of your instructional style, what should be stopped, what should be explained better, and what should be done differently. The exercise takes less than 10 minutes.

FUNCTION

1. Explain that you are a proponent of continuous improvement as well as of customer satisfaction. Because these participants are your customers, and because you are eager to satisfy them by improving the course in every way you can, you would like their written, anonymous feedback at this midway point.

2. Distribute Handout 61-1; allow participants about 5 minutes to respond to the questions.

3. Collect the forms, shuffle them, and then pull one at random. Paraphrase it for the group and advise them of your ability to implement the suggestions. From time to time, select another, read it, and briefly discuss it. (Note: Another option is to save the entire stack, skim it at the break or during lunch, select the top doable priorities, and discuss with the group how you can [or why you can't] put them into effect.)

FOLLOW-UP

Ask someone who has exercised both good judgment and diplomacy to take the evaluations outside the classroom and prepare a summary of recommendations for you. When he or she returns, have the person read the itemized list and respond to each recommendation in terms of your ability to execute it.

Encourage employees to prepare a similar form related to the information most critical to their own job performance, and have their supervisors respond to it.

TRANSITION

I appreciate your willingness to give me feedback about ways we might improve this course. Like all of us, I have my own way of doing things but I'm always open to the possibility there might be a better way. You, too, have your own way of learning. Researchers are always seeking ways to improve that learning process and I hope that you'll be willing to at least try a way that I think will be an improvement over the process you currently use. If you then find your own method is more efficient than mine, by all means, continue with it.

This technique is based on research by cognitive theorist Hilda Taba. She found that when learners first organized the material they were about to receive, they retained it better. So, I'm going to ask that you build broad outlines—advance organizers, she called them—around these five basic points. [Note: The number will depend on how you have organized this particular lecture.]

You can, of course, use the Harvard outline form that you've been using since junior high school. However, you will find your brain more engaged if you use a visual technique. For example, instead of 1, 2, 3, 4, and 5, draw a simple skeleton and take notes in these five outline categories: the head, the hands, and the feet. Or, you might regard this topic as a tree with five branches. Leave lots of room, of course, for note taking. Use any visual you wish, divide it into five broad categories, and get set now to take notes on my lecture.

HANDOUT 61-1

Directions: Please answer the following questions as specifically as possible. Your replies will help us to continuously improve the course.

1. What do you really like about this course so far?_____
_____
_____

2. What do you not like?_____
_____
_____

3. What am I not doing that I should be doing?_____
_____
_____

4. Who or what has been forgotten?_____
_____
_____

5. If you were presenting this training, what would you do differently?_____
_____
_____

6. What questions should be asked?_____
_____
_____

7. What have I given you that you don't want?_____
_____
_____

8. What have I not given you that you would like to have?_____
_____
_____

9. What else would you change?_____
_____
_____

62

CENTENARY CAPSULES

This energizer will stimulate visionary thinking among participants, who are asked to prepare a centenary statement following an instructor-led discussion. This energizer takes about 30 minutes to complete, and includes a handout to be copied and a transparency to be prepared. If possible, obtain canning jars or other glass or plastic containers for encapsulating the vision statements—one for each team of five or six.

FUNCTION

1. Lead a brief discussion citing these points:

- The 100-year anniversary of the establishment of the Dow Jones Index was celebrated on May 29, 1996. The only firm that was originally listed and is still listed today is General Electric. When the company's CEO, Jack Welch, was asked if his firm would be in existence for the 200-year celebration, he responded, "Absolutely!"
- 46 percent (230) of the companies that appeared on the Fortune 500 list in 1980 had disappeared from the list by 1990.
- In less than 20 years, the number of robots being used in the United States went from 32,000 to more than 20,000,000.
- Experts speculate that by the year 2005, 50 percent of all workers will be contingent or part-time or temporary employees.

Ask these questions:

- What from the past will take us into the future?
- What changes do we need to undertake?
- What will work be like 100 years from now?

Refer to these quotations (show Transparency 62-1 now):

- "If the rate of change outside the organization is greater than the rate of change inside the organization, then we are looking at the beginning of the end."—Jack Welch
- "Make no mistake, those who will survive will learn to destroy themselves."—Tom Peters
- "The factory of the future will have only two employees, a man and a dog. The man will be there to feed the dog. The dog will be there to keep the man from touching the equipment."—Warren Bennis

- "When you're through changing, you're through."—Bruce Barton
- "Every new product, process or service begins to become obsolete on the day it first breaks even. Thus, your being the one who makes your product, process or service obsolete is the only way to prevent your competitor from doing so."—Peter F. Drucker
- "Literally the day after my father founded the company [Motorola]…, he had to commence the search for a replacement product…." — Robert Galvin

2.   Divide participants into teams of six or seven and give each a sheet of flip chart paper and a marking pen. Distribute Handout 62-2. Explain that it contains an actual vision statement. The team's task is to prepare a comparable statement for their own organization and to present their thoughts to the remainder of the class. They will have approximately 20 minutes to prepare their statements.

3.   Encapsulate the statements, making certain they are dated and that the names of contributors appear. Discuss creative ways to keep and use the capsules.

FOLLOW-UP

If an organization is approaching a special anniversary, this activity could be conducted organizationwide in the form of a contest, with a prize awarded for the entry that most closely parallels the vision senior management has for the organization's future.

If the participants are same-position employees—all managers, for example, or all support staff members—the assignment could be to describe how the position itself will change in the years ahead.

If you are future-oriented or a techno-buff, provide information from futurists about how life will be lived and business will be conducted 100 years from now. This information could be used to supplement the introduction.

TRANSITION

For those of you involved with strategic planning, for those of you expected to innovate, for those of you wishing to demonstrate leadership, and for those of you seeking ways to effectively manage change, think in terms of five-, ten-, and twenty-year increments for your personal and professional lives and ten-, twenty-, fifty-, and one hundred-year increments for your work units.

No matter what time span you are working with, I think you will find the following information useful, for it presents a skill that transcends time, namely…. [Note: Select for the next segment a skill related to problem solving or effective communications, for example, that has stood and will continue to stand the test of time as far as value is concerned.]

"If the rate of change outside the organization is greater than the rate of change inside the organization, then we are looking at the beginning of the end."

—Jack Welch

"Make no mistake, those who will survive will learn to destroy themselves."

—Tom Peters

"The factory of the future will have only two employees, a man and a dog. The man will be there to feed the dog. The dog will be there to keep the man from touching the equipment."

—Warren Bennis

"When you're through changing, you're through."
—Bruce Barton

"Every new product, process or service begins to become obsolete on the day it first breaks even. Thus, your being the one who makes your product, process or service obsolete is the only way to prevent your competitor from doing so."
—Peter F. Drucker

"Literally the day after my father founded the company [Motorola]..., he had to commence the search for a replacement product...."
—Robert Galvin

HANDOUT 62-2

Read this example and then work with your team to prepare a comparable vision, keeping in mind that *vision* has been described as the ability to see the invisible. What will your organization look like or be like 100 years hence? How will employees differ from today's employees? What work will they be doing and where will they do it? Will your mission and core values remain the same?

The U.S. Small Business Administration (SBA) was created in 1953 as an independent agency of the federal government to aid, counsel, assist and protect the interests of small business concerns, to preserve free competitive enterprise, and to maintain and strengthen the overall economy of our Nation. Small business is critical to our economic recovery, to building America's future, and to helping the United States compete in today's global marketplace.

Our vision for the SBA revolves around two principles: customer-driven outreach and quality-focused management. We are determined to reach out to small businesses in an unprecedented way to listen to their needs, to report these needs back to President Clinton, and to suggest appropriate initiatives to help small businesses. We also recognize the need to change our management culture, our organizational structure, and the way we do business to improve the quality of our work. Through these changes, we will create a more entrepreneurial, customer-driven, and efficient SBA.

As you prepare your vision statement, consider these questions:

> What constants will remain with us for the next 100 years?
> What turbulence can we expect?
> What innovation(s) will we need to ensure continuity into the twenty-first century?

63

TAMING THE TENSION TYRANT

FORM

This energizer is really a skill builder, for it presents strategies by which tension can be reduced at team meetings. Following introductory comments, participants engage in role-play situations in triads. The role plays are designed to encourage deliberate thought instead of reactive responses to conflict. Plan on 30 minutes for this exercise and have the transparency and handout ready in advance.

FUNCTION

1.   Present the following facts and figures and invite reactions.

- The inability to communicate anger appropriately can double the risk of death for people with high blood pressure, according to research done at the University of Michigan.

- Nearly nine out of ten employees experience high stress levels at work once or twice a week.

- Stress costs American organizations over $200 billion a year in mistakes, bad decisions, and lower productivity.

- Violence in the workplace has more than tripled since 1989.

- A survey of 113 corporate recruiters found that employers were most interested in interpersonal skills, ability to solve problems, communications skills, technical knowledge, energy level, and judgment.

- A study by Manchester Partners International found that 40 percent of newly hired or promoted managers fail at their jobs in the first 18 months. The reasons: failure to work on teams, uncertainty about expectations, inability to make tough decisions, and excessive time required to learn.

2.   Continue the discussion via these questions:

- What is the downside to conflict that occurs in team meetings?

- What are some of the positive results than can ensue if conflict is properly channeled?

- What are some strategies for team leaders to employ when conflict occurs? What about team members?

3.   Show Transparency 63-1 and ask for reactions to the quotations:

- "The American people are so tense that it is impossible to put them to sleep—even with a sermon."—Norman Vincent Peale
- "The most important single ingredient in the formula of success is knowing how to get along with people."—Theodore Roosevelt
- "A problem is a chance for you to do your best."—Duke Ellington

4.   Distribute Handout 63-2, which lists 12 options for handling the conflict that erupts at team meetings. Ask participants to check the one they feel would best work for them.

5.   Divide the class into triads. Each triad will engage in three role-plays, with each person rotating through the three roles—the conflict starter, the tension tamer, and the observer. As the basis of the role-plays, they will use the choices they selected from the list of 12. (If there are duplicates, ask the team to make another selection so the three role plays will employ different techniques.)

6.   Upon completion of their role plays, the triads will summarize their insights by preparing a brief report that begins with the sentence, "The next time conflict erupts at a team meeting...."

FOLLOW-UP

As the triads give their reports, a scribe could prepare a master compilation of effective strategies. This list could then be:

- distributed to participants
- posted in meeting rooms
- listed in the company newsletter
- shared with all employees through e-mail
- incorporated in a notebook containing ideas for effective meetings
- posted on bulletin boards with appropriate accompanying cartoons
- distributed to participants in future training sessions dealing with teambuilding, conflict management, and stress.

TRANSITION

Whether you are working in a training session team or in a workplace team, the possibility of tension is always present. Those who know how to tame the tension tyrant know how to build teams more effectively than those without this knowledge. Clearly, conflict management skills are needed in our interpersonal relationships—at a training session, at work, and at home. Such skills can truly reduce the amount of stress each of us is subject to.

You'll forgive me, I hope, for adding a little more stress to your lives with the next portion of this course, a truly challenging segment. But if the stress does overwhelm you, if you find your nerves frayed and your temper getting shorter, at least you'll have some techniques for taming the tension tyrant.

"The American people are so tense that it is impossible to put them to sleep—even with a sermon."

—Norman Vincent Peale

"The most important single ingredient in the formula of success is knowing how to get along with people."

—Theodore Roosevelt

"A problem is a chance for you to do your best."
—Duke Ellington

Directions: Despite the criticisms leveled at meetings, the truth remains that momentous decisions are made when people convene around a common cause. Witness the meeting held in Williamsburg, Virginia in 1774, when George Washington discussed resisting British opposition by force.

Whether we are meeting to attend a training workshop, working in teams on assignments given out during that training, or working in teams at our worksites, whenever two or more people are convened there is the possibility disagreement will occur. Disagreement is actually an expected and valued part of meetings, but when the disagreement becomes out-of-control conflict, little is accomplished.

A.   Review the following 12 suggestions for handling meeting conflict and place a check mark in front of the one you feel would be most useful for you in future meetings.

1.   ❑ Start the meeting with a reminder of the purpose, the mission, the big picture. If appropriate, a nondenominational prayer can be offered.

2.   ❑ Turn around a naysayer's declaration by asking for an explanation. Rather than responding defensively to a statement such as, "That is really a dumb idea," ask instead, "Could you tell me why you think it won't work?" The discussion should then take a more neutral direction.

3.   ❑ For the finger-pointer, have a response such as this ready: "The issue is really not who is to blame, but how we can remedy the situation."

4.   ❑ Admit that some or all of what the other person is saying is true. This may unnerve the attacker so much that he or she will be more willing to work toward compromise.

5.   ❑ The team leader who finds two team members at each other's throats should make an appeal for fairness—fairness on many levels.

6.   ❑ If the disagreement is truly hostile, drop the issue and return to it later.

7.   ❑ Attempt to restate the issue. Clarification of the source of the problem often sets the tone for solution of the problem.

8.   ❑ If you are in the middle of a heated argument (the other person is hot; *you* are cool), call the person by name. This technique is often enough to give the person pause. During the pause, you can interject a meaningful statement, designed to have a soothing effect.

9.   ❑ If the other person is ranting, speak loudly to get his or her attention. Once you have it, speak softly to de-escalate the situation.

10.   ❑ Memorize a quote and repeat it to yourself whenever you find yourself being pulled into an interpersonal conflict. You may even repeat it to the other person as a means of

achieving harmony. A good one is, "It is amazing what ordinary people can do if they set out without preconceived notions."—Charles Kettering

11. ☐ Use the ground rules to control confrontations. If they don't exist, take time (and focus) away from the conflict by establishing ground rules then and there.

12. ☐ If the other person is in a highly emotional state, distract him or her with a comment not related to the situation. Once he or she has regained emotional equilibrium, continue the discussion—but tread lightly.

B.   Now, you will engage in three separate role plays. In one, you will be the observer, sharing your observations when the other two role players finish. In another role play, you will be the tension tamer, gaining practice (as team leader or team member) in the use of one of the preceding 12 suggestions. You will also have the opportunity to play a third role, the role of the conflict starter. Here are some openings you can use to start the conflict.

- That's never going to work.
- I'm tired of hearing you monopolize every meeting.
- You never want to try new ideas.
- I don't know why you're on this team—you're always late, you always leave early, and when you're here, you're always doing something else.
- I'm tired of hearing you complain about management.
- (Supply one of your own.)

64

IF I WERE TO ASK YOU...

FORM

Teamwork is encouraged with this energizer, as participants discuss topic-relevant statistics. They work in teams of five or six to decide the most likely answers to the questions you ask. (Note: The examples used here are for a Women in Leadership workshop. These examples could also work for training in diversity or perhaps sexual harassment. Other statistics should be garnered, however, for other topics. The Form, Function, Follow-Up and Transition will remain the same; only the questions will be different.) Altogether, the exercise takes about 10 minutes. No advance preparation is required, although you may wish to purchase token prizes for the team with the most answers that came near the actual figures.

FUNCTION

1. Find five of the most interesting statistics you can in relation to the course content. Formulate them into questions. For example, a course titled Women in Leadership could use these figures:

- If I were to ask you what the percentage split is between men's names and women's names that appear in the Bible, what would you say? (Answer: 3,037 male names/181 female names = 94% male versus 6% female)

- If I were to ask you what percentage of working women earn half or more than half of the family income, what would you say? (Answer: 64%)

- If I were to ask you what percentage of women do the family chores, what would you say? (Answer: 75%)

- If I were to ask you what percentage of all graduate school enrollees are women, what would you say? (Answer: 53%)

- If I were to tell you that in 1986, the percentage of women in the senior pay level of the federal workforce was 8% and then ask you what the percentage was 10 years later, what would you say? (Answer: 19.2%)

(Note: Keep the articles in which you found the information and have them available for those who would like to see your sources.)

2. Divide the class into teams of five or six. Read them the questions, one at a time, and allow sufficient time for them to decide on their answers.

3. Call on a spokesperson from each team to share their answers as you record them.

4. Reveal the actual statistics and lead a brief discussion regarding them.

5. Congratulate the winning team and award a token prize.

FOLLOW-UP

Select five terms from upcoming instructional modules, terms you are fairly certain participants have never heard before. Then prepare a short quiz, using a format like this example from a workshop in Business Writing. For your information, (b) is the correct answer.

1. The Law of Proximity refers to:

a) The legal principle that asserts distance makes a property owner less likely to maintain property as it should be maintained.

b) The syntactical principle that refers to the location of pronouns as indicative of the antecedents to which they refer.

c) The economic theorem whereby the output of goods and services is in direct proportion to the importance those goods and services have for those in closest proximity to their manufacture.

Invite a local expert to address the class on the topic of the training. In advance, ask him or her to include as many eye-opening statistics as possible in the remarks he or she will make.

TRANSITION

Some of you, I suspect, were truly surprised by these figures. They ran contrary to what you had assumed. They created what psychologists call a cognitive dissonance. When you hear things in the future that oppose what you have come to know or have assumed to know as truth, don't simply reject the possibility because it does not fit neatly into your preestablished constructs. Get rid of the hobgoblins for which little minds are famous.

In this next lecture, you will likely hear some things that go against the grain of your traditional thought. Entertain these things, allow them to penetrate the walls you have established around your knowledge. Perhaps you could even let those walls tumble instead of trying to patch up the cracks new knowledge creates. After all, if you keep on thinking the same thoughts you've always thought, you are not learning." [Note: If possible, select material that runs counter to traditional thinking or the usual way of doing things for the next part of the seminar.]

65

ARE YOU A "SOMEBODY"?

FORM

Using the diagram on the worksheet, you will lead a brief discussion of the types of employees author Charles Handy predicts will populate the organizations of the future. Then, working in groups of three or four, participants will discuss how today's training can make them portfolio people. About 15 minutes will be needed for this energizer.

FUNCTION

1.   Distribute Handout 65-1 and lead a discussion using the questions that appear on the bottom of it.

2.   Have participants form teams of three or four. Each team will discuss at least three specific ways they can use the training they are receiving today to help them become portfolio people.

3.   Each team will select a spokesperson, who will give a brief report on the team's ideas.

4.   Before the reports begin, declare that you want the spokespersons to listen so carefully to the reports that precede their own that they do not repeat anything that has already been said.

5.   Call on the first spokesperson, reminding the others that they should be paying very careful attention, thus developing their listening skills but also saving the class' time by not repeating what's already been said.

FOLLOW-UP

In *Job Shift*, author Bill Bridges talks about a dejobbed future and asserts that if you are fighting for job protection, you're doing nineteenth-century work. The careers of present and future employees will not be on a path of promotions within corporations. Instead, employees will be surfing in the waters of possibilities, looking for the waves that will offer temporary but satisfying accomplishment.

Find reviews of books like *Job Shift*, newspaper articles, magazine pieces—all of which are sounding the same alarms. Make four copies of each and have teams of four work with the various articles to read, discuss, and formulate a written reaction. Then have one four-person team join another team to discuss their respective views.

Have the head of Human Resources discuss his or her views about future work, especially as those views relate to what experts like Bridges are predicting.

TRANSITION

It's been said that the only way to prepare for the future is to invent it. And, it is impossible to invent without knowledge. The more knowledge you have, even if that knowledge is not directly related to the ultimate invention, the more prepared you will be for the future. Already today, you have reviewed or acquired quite a bit of knowledge. [Review at this point some of the major points covered.]

I am being paid to give you as much knowledge as I can, within certain boundaries. Time is one of those boundaries. So we are going to move on to a new chunk of knowledge, this one concerned with _____ [Supply the next topic on the course outline].

Directions: Author Charles Handy foresees the corporation of the future as having employees placed in one of three concentric circles. In the outer circle are those disposable employees, the some-bodies who are usually assigned the work following this sentence, "Well, *somebody* has to do it." In the middle circle are the portfolio people, whose definable skills are so valued that others will want to hire them for a continuous stream of temporary assignments. The core group are those executives (and their wannabe's) who will form the nucleus of the future's virtual organizations. Begin by looking at this diagram depicting the three types of employees:

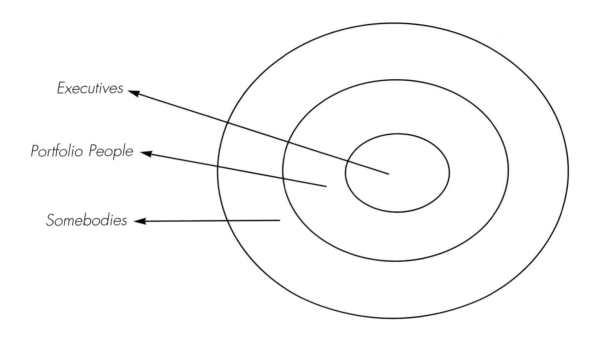

Then consider these questions:

1. How do you feel about Professor Handy's predictions?
2. How can we avoid becoming "somebodies"?
3. Would you rather be an executive or a portfolio person? Explain.
4. If Handy's prediction is accurate, what changes will accompany it?
5. Handy likens portfolio people to actors. Why do you think he has made such an analogy? How would you describe portfolio people?
6. What is your own version of the role employees will play 25 years from now?

Finally, join two or three others. Determine at least three specific ways today's training can help you become portfolio people.

66

EVE & ADAM BOMBS

FORM

This energizer allows participants to switch the tables for a while and to evaluate the trainer's effectiveness. While it takes only moments to execute, the exercise provides valuable insight into your behavior—early enough for you to make calibrations to it if necessary. (Use it around the halfway point in the seminar.) If you are courageous enough to invite further good-natured ribbing, you can even award a prize to the pair that identified the most glaring mistake or "bomb" you made.

FUNCTION

1.   Introduce the exercise this way:

Ever since Eve and Adam bombed in Paradise, we mere mortals have been making mistakes. I make as many as anyone else. Today, I'm going to give you a chance to tell me the most glaring omission, the most serious mistake, the worst thing I said or did. As you think back over what we've covered so far, what would you say was my most serious bomb? Write it down so neither you nor I will forget it."

2.   Divide the group into pairs and have them reflect on your performance thus far and come up with one thing you said or did they think you *should not* have said or done, or one thing you didn't say or do that you *should have* said or done.

3.   Call on each pair to present its opinion. (Note: Don't respond defensively. Instead, try to poke fun at yourself; keep the atmosphere upbeat. You can say something like, "Ouch," or make an exaggerated show of wiping tears from your eyes with a huge hankie, but don't display negative emotions, no matter what you may be feeling.

4.   After each pair has had a chance to express its views, collect their papers and promise you will think more about them. Do!

FOLLOW-UP

Share this popular saying: "We could all retire comfortably if only we could sell our mistakes for what they cost us." Have participants discuss some costly mistakes they have made and then costly mistakes various companies (including their own) have made.

When Buck Rogers took over IBM, he asked every employee what he or she would do if he or she were in charge of the company. The knowledge he gleaned in this way, by his own acknowledgment, helped him immeasurably in the job he had to do. Ask the same question of participants—in terms of the training they receive, the work they do, or the company as a whole.

TRANSITION

When Sam Walton led the Wal-Mart chain, he would encourage employees to "eliminate the dumb." There are things we do just because we have always done them that way. We don't even think about how dumb they may be. So, I thank you for the insights you have provided me today.

Now, the next bit of work we have to do will not be eliminated, ever. That's because the skill I'm about to teach you will make you smart, quite smart indeed when it comes to _____ [Mention the next skill to be presented].

67

GUT RESPONSES/GUTSY RESPONDERS

FORM

The need to base decisions on something more than intuition is reinforced via this energizer, which can be used by individual participants in a class of any size or any number of subgroups composed of five or six members. It will take about 30 minutes for participants to learn how to use this decision-making tool, the F-A-C-T Sheet, which calls for facts and not speculation. Prepare the two transparencies before presenting this exercise.

FUNCTION

1. Hook participants early on by asking, "How many of you make gut decisions?" [Pause.] "How satisfied are you with the results?" [Pause.] "Think of a gut decision you recently made and then think about the outcome. Share that insight with someone sitting near you now."

2. Allow a few minutes for participants to discuss their experiences. Then continue with the lecture.

> Literary critic H. L. Mencken once observed that "for every complex problem, there is one solution that is simple, neat...and wrong." The more complex the problem, the more deserving it is of our full attention and comprehensive study. Sometimes, though, we are tempted to reduce problems to simplistic terms. For example, if I asked you if we should increase the minimum wage, you would no doubt answer in the affirmative, out of concern for low-wage workers.

> But suppose I told you that raising the minimum wage brings with it a whole host of new problems, among them an increased drop-out rate. Would you still be so certain to answer affirmatively? [This counterintuitive challenge to the conventional wisdom is discussed in a Wall Street Journal article, "Higher Minimum Wages, Higher Dropout Rate," by Robert Barro, that appeared in the January 11, 1996, issue.]

> Author Norman Mailer has noted, "There's this faculty in the human mind that hates any question that takes more than ten seconds to answer." Particularly with the immediacy we have come to expect through electronic access to answers, we tend to become impatient quite easily. And so we respond quickly,

sometimes too quickly, to questions and problems that require time and investigation.

What's worse, we often become unshakable in our conviction that our intuitive response is accurate and thus should be used as the basis of the decision. Humorist Will Rogers admonishes us in this regard: "It's not what we don't know that causes trouble. It's what we do know that ain't so!"

As individuals and as team members, we often allow our gut reactions to make decisions for us. This is fine, if we are fairly certain we can trust our intuition. The only way to determine the trustworthiness of our instinct is to assess it. One assessment technique requires you to keep a log of all the decisions you make over a monthlong period. Record each decision and beside it, indicate if the decision is researched (R) and therefore deliberative, or if it is based on intuition (I). As soon as you have the results of a given decision, evaluate the outcome by simply writing (P) for Poor, (A) for Acceptable, or (O) for Outstanding.

At month's end, you will have a good sense of whether or not you are among those rare decision makers who truly have a "golden gut." A majority of Os for the Intuitive decisions is sufficient reason to continue making decisions in this way. But if most of the Os appeared beside the Researched decisions, you would do well to rely more on study than on spontaneity.

Another assessment technique is more immediate. In fact, you will have an opportunity to test the validity of your gut reactions by answering some questions right now. Don't overanalyze the choices, but rather make quick decisions based on your intuitive feelings or gut reactions regarding what the answer should be.

3.   Show Transparency 67-1. (Display the questions one at a time by covering the next question until you feel everyone has had time to answer the current one.)

4.   Share the answers (all "B") and ask participants or table groups, "How well did you do? If you had eight or more B answers, you probably should continue to gauge reality on the basis of what your intuition is telling you. For most of us though, it is altogether too risky to rely on inclination in lieu of facts."

5.   Explain that you have a simple technique, the F-A-C-T Sheet, that invites exploration but does not require months of investigation. For those decisions that we may be tempted to make intuitively, the F-A-C-T Sheet invites a fuller exploration of the issue yet does not require an inordinate amount of time.

6. Before showing the transparency, ask a simple question such as, "Should we end class an hour earlier today?" The first reaction, the gut response of participants, would be to shout "Yes" resoundingly. But gutsy responders, true leaders, would go against the affirmative tide by asking team members to consider the question more carefully. The F-A-C-T Sheet tames unbridled enthusiasm so that decisions can be considered dispassionately. It is not always popular to ask a group to set passions aside, but if the gut is blocking the brain in the decision-making process, the F-A-C-T technique is all the more necessary.

7. Show Transparency 67-2.

8. Ask participants to reconsider the "Should-we-get-out-early?" question from the F-A-C-T perspective.

9. Wrap up the exercise with a discussion of the decision-making process. These questions will prompt significant exchanges.

- How many decisions do you make a day? What is an example of a meaningful decision? A meaningless decision? A mindless decision? A mission-related decision?
- What process do you use for decision making?
- Do you seek or use the opinions of others as you make decisions?
- Do you tend to use either/or choices?
- How do you know when you have made the right decision?
- How are organizational or strategic decisions made at your place of work? (If you do not have access to this information, consider how those decisions *should* be made.)
- What, in your experience, is a decision that backfired?
- On what assumptions does your manager make decisions?
- How are the consequences of poor decisions addressed in your work environment?

FOLLOW-UP

To reinforce the learning, cite the course objectives again, and ask each participant to work with a partner and tell that person what he or she has learned from this exercise in relation to the objectives.

This exercise could be adapted to virtually any course by substituting topic-relevant questions for the quiz. As it stands, the exercise works well with problem-solving, teambuilding, supervision, leadership, and decision-making classes.

TRANSITION

Although it is harder to use facts than the fiction of our own infallibility, you as a decision maker owe it to yourself and to those who will be impacted by your decisions to allocate both time and resources to the decision-making process. Yes, there are some people with a "golden gut" when it comes to being decisive. But those individuals are few and far between.

Having said all of that, I must tell you that I have a gut feeling that you are in the mood for some serious learning. Rather than relying on a F-A-C-T sheet to find out if I'm right, I think I'll just trust my instinct and move right into our next task.

1) How many Americans of voting age are *not* registered to vote?
    a) 11 million
    b) 64 million
    c) 82 million

2) The city with the most immigrants in the world is:
    a) London
    b) Toronto
    c) Los Angeles

3) The percentage of victims of violent crime who know the attacker is:
    a) 14%
    b) 41%
    c) 72%

4) Food poisoning costs how much a year for treatment and lost productivity?
      a) $22 million
      b) $22 billion
      c) $2.2 trillion

5) Within three hours during the 1989 U.S. Open, three golfers had holes-in-one on the 6th hole at Oak Hill in Rochester, New York. The odds of that happening are:
      a) 1.2 million to 1
      b) 2.4 million to 1
      c) 24 million to 1

6) An Accountemps survey found bosses spend what percent of their management time resolving personality conflicts?
      a) 8%
      b) 18%
      c) 28%

7) A Day-Timers survey found how many Americans using lists to keep organized?
      a) 63%
      b) 84%
      c) 93%

8) 81% of all sales are closed after
      a) the first call
      b) the fifth call
      c) the seventh call

9) The "Little Red Elephant" is
      a) a children's story
      b) a synonym for lousewort
      c) the name of a Malaysian ballet

10) How long can you survive without water?
      a) 24 hours
      b) 72 hours
      c) 5 days

F <u>OCUS</u> What is our true focus here? What are the intents surrounding this decision?

A <u>DDITIONS</u> What additional perspectives, facts, or viewpoints should be considered here? What may we be overlooking?

C <u>ONSEQUENCES</u> What are some possible ramifications of this decision? Who or what might be negatively impacted?

T <u>RADE-OFFS</u> How else could we achieve our aim? What would we be willing to relinquish?

CLOSERS

68

STRATIFIED SUMMARIES

FORM

This is actually a two-part activity. The first, a mental challenge, sets the stage for the second, which requires a list of remembered points and then a stratification of the list. In all, the lesson requires 30–45 minutes. Participants will work in small groups of four or five.

For the first part, you will need an overhead projector for Transparency 68-1. If flip charts are available, they work well with the second assignment. If not, participants can do the task using paper and pencils.

FUNCTION

1.   Form groups of four or five and explain that the brainteaser will be used as a segue to a summarization exercise:

Before we begin to wrap up, I'd like to engage your minds with a brainteaser. I'm going to give you three words or phrases and ask that you think of a fourth word, which, when placed before or after each of the three words or phrases, will complete a familiar phrase.

For example, if the three entries were cat and pad and church, the missing fourth word (that would apply to all three of the others) would be mouse. Or, if the words or phrases were break, purple, and soul, the answer would be heart. Are there any questions? If not, work in your group but keep your voices down so the other groups don't hear your answers.

Once we've completed this exercise, we'll do a similar one to summarize the day's learnings.

2.   Show the transparency and allow about 5 minutes for completion.

3.   Supply the answers:

1 = table		6 = shock	
2 = star		7 = flat	
3 = clock		8 = head	
4 = coast		9 = jump	
5 = duty		10 = low	

4.   Continue with the lecture:

When we find a common thread among seemingly disparate pieces of information, we are engaging in a process known as stratification. The process offers us a way to analyze emerging trends. It is an excellent tool for teams working to solve problems and make improvements.

Now, I want you, still working in the same groups, to make as long a list as possible of everything you remember learning since the moment class began. Try not to look at your notes— or at anyone else's notes! Don't look in your books or at any handouts. Instead, with one person recording, pool your collective thoughts about the things we have discussed, the topics we have covered, the knowledge you have gained. Create a master list, with one person writing but all of you contributing. You should be able to compile a list of 30 topics within the next ten to fifteen minutes. [Allow time for this.]

Now comes the hard part. I'm going to ask that you stratify the list. That is, you are going to come up with four to six stratifications or broad categories within which each of the 30 topics can be placed. Some topics may fit into more than one category. [Give an illustration. In a class on listening, for example, one category might be Psychological and in it might be words such as preconceptions or fear or stress.] Some of the topics may be related to theories or to statistics, to people or to events, to quotations or to definitions. We've covered a great deal in the last day [Adjust to course duration]. See how much you can remember.

5.   Allow about 10 minutes. Circulate among the groups to assist as needed.

6.   Conclude the lecture:

We do not absorb information in the same linear fashion in which it is presented. Our brains sort through the information and certain things stand out to certain persons for certain reasons. So, when we attempt to recall what we have learned, the knowledge has often become quite jumbled—as you saw when you were compiling the lists.

Stratification, though, will help you get a handle on these disparate chunks of knowledge. When you go to work tomorrow and a coworker asks, "What did you learn yesterday?" it will be much easier to relay the four or five stratified categories than the crazy disconnects that appeared on the original list. Let's find out now what some of those categories were.

7.   Call on each table group to share its stratifications.

When participants return to the workplace, they can apply the stratification tool to meetings. At the end of each meeting, the team leader or facilitator takes 5 minutes to ask people, individually, to recall what was covered during the course of the meeting. Then the lists are stratified so main topics can be translated into minutes or shared informally with those not in attendance.

Stratification is also useful during the problem-solving process. Encourage participants to periodically (working alone or in a team) list all the possible causes of a given effect and then to stratify them. Such detailing prevents latching onto the most likely cause of a problem and encourages greater and wider deliberation instead.

Periodically, we need to reflect on the learning we have acquired. It is hard to absorb our hard-won knowledge unless we have a reflective time during which to consider it. For example, we have covered quite a bit of material today. If I asked you to organize that material into three broad categories, what would you call them? [Elicit several suggestions. Then select an appropriate one, and conclude:] *Write these three categories on a card. Refer to it periodically. Write down as much as you can remember in each category from this training program. Each time you engage in this sort of review, try to better your best recall. In other words, if you remembered 18 things from the last review, try to reach 20 on the next.*

1. setting   manners   tennis

2. movie   power   fish

3. watcher   alarm   radio

4. west   guard   along the

5. jury   free   patriotic

6. absorbers   treatments   insulin

7. ware   foot   "B"

8. ache   band   hunter

9. off   shot   bail

10. life   key   pressure

69

LIGHTS, CAMERA, FRACTIONS

FORM
Team captains withdraw fractional elements of the course length, determine the most important events that occurred during that time, and then write a script for a video depicting the sequences of salient learning moments. The actual writing will take about 30 minutes. The handout provides critical considerations for the script writers; duplicate it in advance of this closing activity. Use fractions that fit with both the size of the group and the length of the course.

FUNCTION

1.   Write appropriate fractions on separate sheets of paper and place the papers in an envelope. For a one-day program of eight hours, for example, you could use: 1/8; 1/4; 3/8; 1/2; 5/8; 3/4; 7/8; 8/8. (The fractions will vary, depending on course length, course hours, and your own preference for dividing the time blocks.)

2.   Ask eight volunteers to withdraw one slip of paper each. These eight will first serve as captains of their small teams. (Later, they will work as co-captains when each team joins one other team.)

3.   The eight writing captains will select others to be on their writing team.

4.   Distribute the handout and allow about one-half hour for the writers to outline their video.

5.   After about 15 minutes, the smaller-fraction writing teams and their captains (1/8 team, for example) will join with their next-in-line fraction team. The captains will now serve as co-captains. (The 1/8 team, then, will join the 1/4 team. The remaining team combinations will be 3/8 with 1/2; 5/8 with 3/4; and 7/8 with 8/8.)

6.   After the combined teams have worked for 15 minutes, call on each of the four larger-fraction captains (1/4, 1/2, 3/4, and 8/8) to review the elements that would be included in their segment. This review simultaneously serves as a sequential summary of the course in its entirety. If salient points are omitted during this review, feel free to add them.

FOLLOW-UP
Show a short video on a topic relevant to the training, twice. The first time, participants will view it for the purpose of gleaning information per-

tinent to the course. The second time they will view it from a cinematic perspective, to pick up pointers they can include in their own scripts.

Determine if anyone is interested in making a short video, highlighting the essential training points and including interviews with course participants. If so, encourage the pursuit of such a project, employing the actual scripts participants have created.

TRANSITION

Because you are drenched in so much data by the end of a workshop such as this, it is often difficult to put the knowledge in its proper perspective. By framing it into a sequential series of events, such as we have done with these scripts, it is easier to order our thoughts and to remember all that we actually know. I hope you will find these scripts useful as you outline the learning events that took place during these last eight hours [Substitute appropriate time].

HANDOUT 69-1

Think about the important concepts that were presented or things that occurred at various points in this training program. Then work with others to incorporate those essential elements into a script. Let these recommendations guide you.

1.   Begin by brainstorming as long a list as you can (use your notes, too) of ideas that were discussed, points that were made, and things that happened during the time period reflected in your fraction.

2.   Now decide the format you will use: narrator, interviews, all visuals, or a setting (such as a courtroom). Will you fashion the script as a mystery, as a romance, or as a problem that appears throughout the video? Will you use vignettes or music? Will you have a main character who appears in virtually every scene? Let your creativity guide you as you make these and other decisions.

3.   Before you begin writing, decide on the tone: Will you take a humorous approach, an entirely factual approach, a docudrama style?

4.   Start with a bang. Capture the audience's attention as soon as you can.

5.   Make sure the dialogue is consistent with the people who are speaking it. Is it smooth? Is it realistic?

6.   Your plot line should be interesting enough to keep your viewers hooked. If possible, include subplots that run beneath the surface.

7.   Ask yourself:

> What is my main message here?
>
> Is it presented in a logical fashion or does it seem disjointed?
>
> What visual effects can help me convey this message?
>
> What structure will I use?
>
> How will I review the main points made?
>
> What would make viewers think, "I really learned something from this"?

70

SWEET SEVENTEEN

FORM

Large teams of seven or eight participants split this assignment: Half work on a brainteaser and the other half list 17 specific points they have learned during the training session. This closer takes about 10 minutes to complete and requires copies of the worksheet, flip chart paper, and marking pens for each team.

FUNCTION

1. Divide the group into teams of seven or eight.

2. Distribute Handout 70-1.

3. While half of each team is working on the puzzle, the other half will be listing 17 specific details from the training that is now drawing to a close.

4. After about 10 minutes, show the answer (Transparency 70-1).

FOLLOW-UP

Post the lists and work with the whole group to create a prioritized list of the most relevant or valuable knowledge, skills, and abilities they acquired.

Videotape the reports and reassemble participants three months later to view it. Discuss how they are using the knowledge, skills, and abilities they learned or developed during the seminar.

TRANSITION

Ideally, you have learned more than seventeen things as a result of the hard work you have put into this training session. Depending on the nature of your jobs and the prior knowledge you brought to the class, various skills or pieces of information will mean more to some of you than to others. Decide for yourself how you can best use this new knowledge. Commit to making a return on the investment that has been made in you.

HANDOUT 70-1

Directions: Half the people in your team will work on the following puzzle:

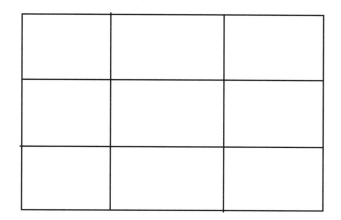

The object is to put an odd number in each empty square so that each row (whether across, down, or diagonal) adds up to 27. Select from these numbers: 1, 3, 5, 7, 9, 11, 13, 15, 17. Do not use any number more than once.

While half of you are working on this puzzle, the other half will list 17 of the most valuable things you learned from this training.

1. _____
2. _____
3. _____
4. _____
5. _____
6. _____
7. _____
8. _____
9. _____
10. _____
11. _____
12. _____
13. _____
14. _____
15. _____
16. _____
17. _____

11	1	15
13	9	5
3	17	7

71

THE RING OF SPORTS

FORM

This closer requires some creative expression as participants, working in groups of four or five, select one sports-related image and explain how and why that particular image relates to the training they have received. The exercise, including the team reports, takes about 15 minutes to complete. The only thing you need do to prepare for it is to make copies of the handout.

FUNCTION

1. Distribute Handout 71-1. Give participants a moment or two to look it over and to begin thinking about their selections.

2. Divide the group into teams of four or five. Each team will select one sports image, list the terms related to it, and then prepare a brief report explaining its choices.

3. After 5–10 minutes, ask each team to give its report.

FOLLOW-UP

Extending the sports allusions, have participants make up rules for optimizing the training. For example, to have a home run, they will have to cover three bases....

Invite a professional or semiprofessional athlete or coach to address the group about the importance of practice and persistence in achieving self- or other-imposed goals.

TRANSITION

Sometimes, by placing content in an atypical context, we are able to view it in new ways. I hope you have gleaned some new insights by way of examining your training from an athletic perspective. In fact, if you hope to bat a thousand in your efforts to put your training to good use, you will probably be disappointed.

Nonetheless, you can have slam-dunk success by resolving to use at least one of these ideas within the first twenty-four hours of your return to work.

Directions: As a team, choose one sports-related image from the ring of possibilities below.

Now, think of as many terms as possible related to that sport.

_____   _____   _____

_____   _____   _____

_____   _____   _____

_____   _____   _____

Finally, write a short paragraph, using the terms above, to explain the significance of the training you have had and its relevance to the work you do. _____

_____

_____

_____

_____

_____

_____

72

SLO-MO SOW; GROW

FORM

Participants work alone on this closer, taking about 10 minutes to reflect on and review the success they've had with this training program.

FUNCTION

1.   Ask participants to get comfortable and to clear their minds of distracting thoughts.

2.   Now ask them to think of a time in their lives when they were in a high-performance mode, a time when success was in their grasp. Large or small accomplishments are equally acceptable.

3.   As they relive these feel-good moments of the past, ask them to recall the factor(s) that led to the achievement: Was it perseverance? Was it the support of colleagues, friends, family? Was it the help of a coach or mentor? Was it that they were on a winning streak?

4.   Have them continue moving backward in time to the point that actually kicked off the chain of events that resulted in the success they had many months or many years later.

5.   Liken the training they are completing to that starting point. Encourage them to move through the chain of events so they can, in time, experience more accomplishments like the ones they are now reliving.

FOLLOW-UP

Have participants share their memories with one another in class and with colleagues when they go back to work. Have them transition, in these shared accounts, from past to future success via present efforts.

Suggest that participants form a study group to continue the glory moments. They might meet on a regular basis and find ways to keep alive the flush-with-learning-success moments.

TRANSITION

We've all known success in one form or another—at work, at home, in school, on the playing field. But we tend to remember the ultimate manifestation only. We submerge, typically, the long hours and hard work that preceded the final results. You have worked very hard to learn what I taught. In a sense, though, the hard work is just beginning. It is up to you now to convert these theories into actual practice. I have given you the tools. How you take care of them and what you build with them is entirely within your power from this point on. I can only say, "More power to you!"

73

BIZARRELY COMMITTED

FORM

Based on a Tom Peters allusion to "wildly enthusiastic, bizarrely committed" individuals, participants will compose a list of words and deeds that evince such descriptions of learners in a training situation. The closer, which takes about 10 minutes and has participants working in teams of three or four, can be extended by asking which participants have shown some of the traits on the list.

FUNCTION

1. Begin with this mini-lecture.

   Apathy is a dangerous thing. As the spirit erodes, so does productivity and, in time, the very will to work. Fortunately, in this room over the last two days [Supply appropriate length of time.] we have seen behaviors that are anything but apathetic. In fact, the interest I've seen here has been what Tom Peters would call "wildly enthusiastic" and even "bizarrely committed." He uses these descriptors in the job ads he places.

   Think about yourself as a learner. [Pause.] Take a look around this room at your fellow learners. [Pause.] Think about what would be said and done—what has been said and done—by people enthusiastic about and committed to acquiring new knowledge.

2. Divide the class into teams of three or four.

3. Allow about 5 minutes for them to compile a list of things that would be said and done by learners who were wildly enthusiastic about this training topic and who were bizarrely committed to applying the training to their workplace situations. They should have at least ten items on their lists. Encourage them to use specific examples of what has transpired in the classroom.

4. Ask someone from the first team to read the team's list. Have the other teams follow suit.

FOLLOW-UP

Have participants select three of the descriptive terms and write a contract to exhibit these positive behaviors in the future. The contract should be signed by you, by the participant, and, if at all possible, by the participant's supervisor.

Compile a master list of these traits, type it up, and pass it out to future attendees, with a heading at the top such as, "Sound like anyone you know?" Use the list to introduce your expectations for participants at the very beginning of the next course.

TRANSITION

I realize it is difficult to maintain the momentum you are now experiencing. When we return to work, life has a way of intruding upon our plans, despite our best intentions. Somehow, it is easier to return to business as usual than to make our work unusual. Inertia is a powerful barrier to change.

It would be a shame if the plans you have made to continue learning, to refine your skills, to keep in touch, to introduce change were abandoned. I believe, however, that if your will is strong enough, you can have your way.

74

WORST-CASE SCENARIOS

FORM

Participants think of the worst learning moments they have ever experienced, going all the way back to their elementary school years and continuing to the present. They then share those moments and use them as a basis for evaluating the training that is now drawing to a close. This closer takes about 10 minutes and requires no materials or advance preparation other than duplicating the handout.

FUNCTION

1. Ask participants to sit together in teams of three or four.

2. Have them reflect on their learning experiences, beginning in first grade and moving through junior high, high school, college, perhaps even graduate school and on-the-job training. In view of all the learning they have acquired in all those years, ask them which experiences stand out in their minds as the worst ever. Allow about 5 minutes for discussion.

3. Merge the smaller teams so that new groups of six to eight members are formed.

4. Distribute Handout 74-1 and have participants evaluate the training that is nearly finished by comparing it to the worst-case scenarios they have experienced.

FOLLOW-UP

Continue the exercise by having participants recall best-case learning scenarios and comparing those to the current training as well.

Lead a discussion of worst-case scenarios from the actual workplace. Then elicit suggestions on how this training could be utilized in such worst-case circumstances.

TRANSITION

I certainly hope you will regard much of what we have done as best-case scenarios. We have had optimal experiences— an environment conducive to learning; a group that was serious about acquiring new knowledge and new experiences; materials that captured the course content and that will serve as a future resource; and enough time to cover the topic in depth.

When you attempt to effect change next week, based on what you have learned, the conditions will probably not be optimal.

This is where your perseverance will come in. If you are determined to make use of this information, you can and you will. But, at least at first, your struggle will probably be an uphill struggle. I have confidence that you will ultimately meet each other, though, on top of these metaphoric mountains of achievement.

Directions: In the blank spaces on the left-hand side of each continuum line, write succinct but substantial descriptions of the worst training experiences you and your teammates have ever had. If possible, categorize these incidents with labels such as Environment, Instructor, Materials, Other participants, Time factor, et cetera.

Then, compare the training you have been participating in to the worst circumstances you, collectively, have known. Use 0 to represent the worst-case setting and 10 the ideal. (Request a second sheet if you have more than five scenarios.)

1. Worst-case
   incident

   _____
   _____
   _____
   _____

   Category:

   _____

   | 0   1   2   3   4   5   6   7   8   9   10 |

2. Worst-case
   incident

   _____
   _____
   _____
   _____

   Category:

   _____

   | 0   1   2   3   4   5   6   7   8   9   10 |

3. Worst-case
   incident

   _____
   _____
   _____
   _____

   Category:

   _____

   | 0   1   2   3   4   5   6   7   8   9   10 |

4. Worst-case
   incident

   _____
   _____
   _____
   _____

   Category:

   _____

   | 0   1   2   3   4   5   6   7   8   9   10 |

5. Worst-case
   incident

   _____
   _____
   _____
   _____

   Category:

   _____

   | 0   1   2   3   4   5   6   7   8   9   10 |

75

LESSONS LEARNED

FORM

In this closer activity, each person thinks about and notes the lessons he or she has learned, using the transparency to guide that thinking. Small groups then share their thoughts. Finally, you will call upon a few participants at random to disclose what they have learned. The closer takes about 15 minutes and requires nothing in the way of preparation beyond making the transparency.

FUNCTION

1.   Note that because the course is drawing to a close, now is a good time to think back over what participants have learned—and not only about the training topic.

2.   Show Transparency 75-1 and ask them to make notes as you show each of the questions. Pause while they write, then show the next one.

3.   Have participants work in groups of four or five to discuss their answers to these questions.

4.   Randomly, call on a few people to share their thoughts.

FOLLOW-UP

Ask each group to prepare a synthesis of their responses. Put these on audiotape and keep the tape in the company library for other learners to hear.

Suggest that participants set up interview appointments with learning leaders in their organizations—that is, those who have effectively managed to persuade others to adopt a new process, a new practice, a new way of doing things or thinking about things. Having gleaned as many tips as possible from their interviewees, participants should then attempt to emulate at least one successful technique.

TRANSITION

My purpose for being here, of course, has been to teach you about this topic. But learning does not occur in a vacuum. As you were learning about this subject, you were also learning about yourself, about others, about what you will do with the learning you have acquired. Use these insights as you put this new knowledge to good use. Think about the circumstances, the fear that surrounds change, and the persuasion you will need to use with your coworkers as you put your action plans into effect.

What have you learned about this subject?

What have you learned about yourself?

What have you learned about your fellow learners?

What have you learned about group dynamics?

What have you learned about how this training could best be put to use?

76

WIGGLE GIGGLES

FORM

Participants relate graphics shown on transparencies to the way they feel they conducted themselves during the course of the training and how they *will* conduct themselves once the training is complete. You then offer psychological insights into their choices. The value of this closer, which takes 5–10 minutes to complete, lies in the reflection it engenders as participants think about what they have learned and how they will use it. A group dynamics bonus is the laughter that is produced as participants learn the "interpretations" of their choices. Make transparencies for each of the five questions.

FUNCTION

1. Explain that ever since the popularization of Hermann Rorschach's ink blots, psychologists have been interested in learning how people think by analyzing how they view visual images. Now that the course is nearly over, you would like participants to reflect on their behavior as learners. Show Transparency 76-1 now and ask them to write down the letter of the image they feel best represents how they felt at first.

2. Point out that, as people become acclimated to their circumstances, their concerns about fitting in recede to the background and their desire to learn moves to the foreground. Next have them view themselves as learners during the first half of the class. Which image on Transparency 76-2 best reflects their attitudes and behaviors during that time? Again, they will record their answers.

3. Once people have established a comfortable modus operandi, they tend to continue with it unless something or someone gives them good reason to change. Ask them, in retrospect, what kind of learners they were in the second half of the class. Show Transparency 76-3 as you do so. Have them write down their choices.

4. Explain that upon completion of the training, they will be expected to serve as idea-warriors, taking information back to the workplace and using it to effect positive change. As you display Transparency 76-4, they will select the image that best represents how they see themselves performing when they return to work.

5. Finally, ask them to think about themselves one year from today. Which image best reflects the way they way they see themselves working, thinking, and learning in the future? Show Transparency 76-5 and have them record their answers.

6. Keep one transparency at a time showing and ask participants to tally their answers and then to work in dyads or triads, sharing their choices and the reasons behind them.

7. After several minutes of discussion, reveal the psychological interpretations:

If they had three or more "a" answers, they have a tendency to welcome new experiences, embrace the unusual, take risks, and try new things.

If they had three or more "b" answers, they are likely to seek harmony as they interact with other people. Typically, people with a majority of "b" answers give of themselves, express themselves openly, and trust their instincts to do the right thing.

If they had three or more "c" answers, they are extraverted individuals, who enjoy being in charge and who do not hesitate to take a leadership role. "C" responders are known as self-starters, individuals who have goals and who meet them.

Studiously avoid talking about a majority of "d" answers. Typically, someone will ask for the "d" interpretation. Act embarrassed. Hem and haw. Look around the room. Avoid eye contact. Pretend that only with great reluctance are you willing to share what having three or more "d" answers really means: that the person is oversexed!

8. When the laughter dies down, reveal that the real purpose of the exercise was to have them think about their attitudes and actions as learners at various stages of the learning experience. The interpretations were not serious and are not to be given any credibility at all.

FOLLOW-UP

Obtain a copy of the video *Psychogeometrics* (produced by Etc./Career-Track) to learn more about how visual selections reflect psychological inclinations.

Suggest that participants read *Who Do You Think You Are?* by Keith Harary and Eileen Donahue. This book and others offer true psychological insights into the way we work, think, learn, act, and interact with others.

TRANSITION

Even though this exercise was not intended to be a serious assessment of your learning style, it was intended to make you think...to make you think about your basic learning style, and about how and when, where and with whom you can continue this journey. You have the road map now—all you need is to define your destination and then take the first step toward reaching it.

Which image best represents how you felt the first few minutes you were here?

a) 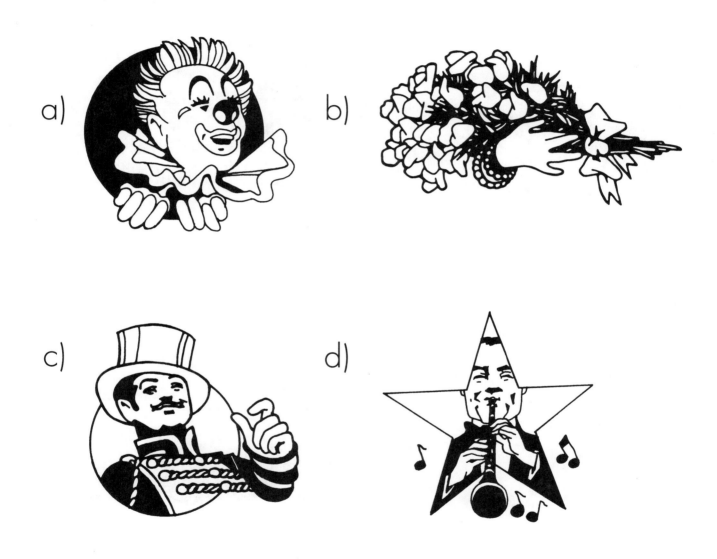 b)

c) d)

Which image best captures your attitudes and behaviors during the first half of this training program?

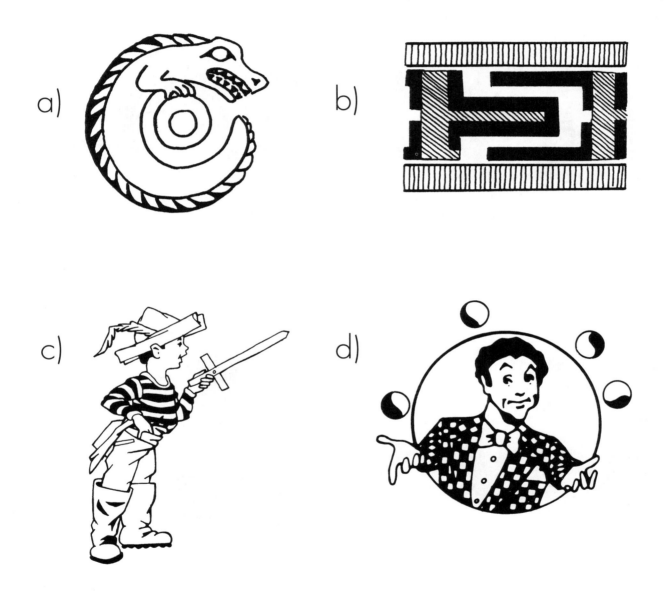

Which image best represents you as a learner during the second half of this training?

a)

b)

c)

d)

Which image reflects the way you will operate upon your return to work?

a)

b)

c)

d)

Which image best embodies you as you will be working, thinking, learning one year from today?

a)

b)

c)

d)

77

NEXT STEPS

FORM

This closer asks participants to complete the steps that will lead to the fullest implementation of the new knowledge they have acquired. Using the handout that you have duplicated in advance, participants will list specific actions to be taken in order to achieve posttraining success as they define it. Participants work alone on this exercise, which takes about 5 minutes to complete.

FUNCTION

1.   Give a brief introduction such as this:

Knowledge that is not used is knowledge wasted. The time, money, effort, and other resources that have gone into giving you this gift of knowledge will be lost unless you plan to use that knowledge to make some improvements in the way work is done or meetings are held or communications are exchanged. [Note: Other examples may be even more appropriate here.]

Until now, we have been focusing on knowledge acquisition. Now, however, it is time to think about knowledge application.

2.   Ask, "In your opinion, what posttraining results would make this training successful? If you owned this company, what evidence would convince you that this training has been worth the resources put into it?"

3.   Distribute Handout 77-1, which asks participants to define what posttraining success would look like. Given this definition, participants will then specify the steps that would lead to this success.

4.   Call upon at least four people to share their success steps with the group.

FOLLOW-UP

If possible, have the supervisors of participants present for informal discussions of how to implement these next steps by partnering. Such discussions lend a legitimacy and seriousness to the plans participants have formulated and will help move those plans closer to becoming organizational realities.

If there is a common conference room, post the worksheets there and invite input from others. If no such room is available, ask permission to set up a temporary bulletin board in a well-traveled corridor. Again, invite passers-by to comment on the plans laid out.

TRANSITION

You've no doubt heard it said that the journey of a thousand miles begins with a single step. There is another proverb, this a Japanese one, that says you can know ten things by learning one. The things you have learned today [Substitute appropriate time reference] have, I suspect, given you new insights, new cognitive constructs, new knowledge. For example, as you contemplate what to do with what you have learned, you probably realize the implementation stage will not be easy. You probably also know that without some plan detailing the steps, the implementation might not even occur. Use these worksheets, refer to them often, and let them inspire you to continuously move forward.

HANDOUT 77-1

Directions: Assume you are the person in your organization who determines the worth of training that is provided to employees. As you examine the costs, you no doubt ask yourself, "What do we have to show for these expenditures?" Now answer your own question: "If you were this person, what would you need to *see* to prove to you these expenditures should continue to be made?" Write your definition of post-training success here:_____

_____

_____

_____

Now, in view of this definition, tell what specific steps participants would have to take in order to make this definition a reality. Write the necessary actions beside the footsteps.

Step 1   _____

_____

_____

Step 2   _____

_____

_____

Step 3

_____

_____

_____

Step 4   _____

_____

_____

Step 5

_____

_____

_____

SUCCESS

78

BEST-IN-CLASS OUTPUTS

FORM

Working in triads on this closer, participants will decide what was one of the best parts of the training and will then create an output based on that identified segment. The outputs will be used by the participants themselves, by their coworkers, and by others who attend future training programs on this topic. They will need about 15 minutes for this exercise.

FUNCTION

1. Ask participants to form triads and to decide what they considered the best part of the class, in terms of an idea or skill that was presented.

2. Next ask them to think of a product they could create that would help future learners acquire and use that knowledge or that skill. The output they will create could be something like a study guide or a self-assessment tool related to the information they identified as having been so valuable. It could be in the form of a list of Do's and Don'ts or a Five-Step Process for learning.

Triads may want to immortalize themselves by giving their output a name, such as the Jomarken Approach to Making Effective Decisions (compiled by Joseph, Martine, and Ken). Participants may wish to prepare something like the Supervisor's Ten Commandments or the Office Professional's Bill of Rights. Other possibilities might be the Salesperson's Checklist for Cold Calls, the Team Leader's Guide to Effective Meetings, or the Seven Habits of Highly Effective Speakers.

FOLLOW-UP

Ask for a volunteer from each triad to type up their product and to return it to you for subsequent duplication and distribution to all participants. You could also send copies to the supervisors of those in attendance.

For a period of 5 minutes, have newly formed triads brainstorm all the possible ways these products could be put to good and profitable use.

TRANSITION

By creating this product, you have concretized information; you have made it conform to your own needs. With this product, you now have a tangible means of transferring theory to practice and practice into perfection. Use these products, give them to coworkers, and let these good ideas evoke even better ideas in the future.

79

CERTIFIABLE

FORM

This closer requires certificates of completion, either those officially distributed by the organization or those you create on a computer. Each participant receives a certificate with someone else's name on it and is then required to write a short presentation speech to deliver as he or she presents the certificate to the other member. It is best to use this closer with a relatively small class, as you will need approximately 1 minute per participant plus about 5 minutes for the actual speech writing. (Speeches can be as short as two sentences.) Have the transparency ready for them to refer to as they write their speeches.

FUNCTION

1.   Pass out the certificates, ensuring that no one receives his or her own.

2.   Ask participants to write a short presentation speech, to be delivered when they present the certificates to their rightful owners. The tips on Transparency 79-1 should be helpful.

3.   After 5 minutes, begin the presentation process, by which the first person gives the certificate to (and delivers the speech about) the person whose name is on the certificate. That person then does the same for the person whose certificate he or she is holding. The process continues until each person has received a certificate and has had a short speech delivered about him or her.

FOLLOW-UP

If time permits, have the recipients say a few words (other than "thank you") as a short acceptance speech.

Encourage participants to continue with such recognition ceremonies and celebrations when they return to the workplace. Even if they are not supervisors, they can certainly engage in peer recognition efforts.

TRANSITION

Now that you have your certificates of completion, you probably think the course is over. Wrong! You're not getting out of here until I commend you once more for your seriousness and your studiousness in plowing through this material, much of which was quite complex. You have truly accomplished quite a bit. The next time I see you, and the next time you see one another, be ready to talk about how you are actually using the information you have been storing up throughout the session.

What stands out in your mind about the person whose certificate you are holding? (Can you use a quote in reference to him or her?)

Even if you did not have a chance to work with this person, tell what you think the person may be like—as an employee, as a learner, as a thinker, maybe even as a trainer for part of this course.

How do you foresee this person using the knowledge he or she has gained?

What might this person be doing in 5 years? How will he or she be using this training?

80

DESIGNER GLEANS

FORM

Participants will work with one other person on this closer, which asks them to design a final exam based on the most salient points they have gleaned from the training just concluded. They will need at least 15 minutes for this exercise.

FUNCTION

1. Divide the class into pairs.

2. Start with these directions:

Not all educators believe in the effectiveness of final exams, but most tests do reveal, at least to some extent, what the learner has learned. Now that we are only minutes away from the completion of this course, I'm going to ask you not to take a final exam, but to make a final exam. Reflect with your partner on all the material that has been covered. Then, chooose what you feel are the most pertinent points and design a ten-question examination.

3. After 10 minutes, call on one pair at a time to read the questions they have prepared slowly, repeating each and allowing time for the other participants to respond.(This closer could be quite time-consuming in a large class. You may prefer to have each pair ask only one or two questions.)

FOLLOW-UP

Have pairs give their exams to other pairs, who will take the exams and then confer with the test makers to learn if their answers were correct.
On a lighter note, present Handout 80-1 and ask pairs to fill it in.

TRANSITION

The real measure of success with this training is not how well you do on exams, of course, but rather how well you use the knowledge in the future. If you can help others because of some new ideas you have taken in or have generated while sitting here, if you can improve processes, if you can defuse hostility or streamline meetings [Supply appropriate terms], *then, indeed, you have passed the course.*

Directions: Below you will see the brain of someone who has just completed this course. Working with your partner, fill in each area of the brain to reflect the thoughts that are probably in this person's head right now. Use both broad brush strokes and fine brush strokes to reflect his or her cerebellum categories: Put a label on each of the cerebellum sections and then supply a few examples of the kinds of thoughts that would be in each section. One has been done for you.

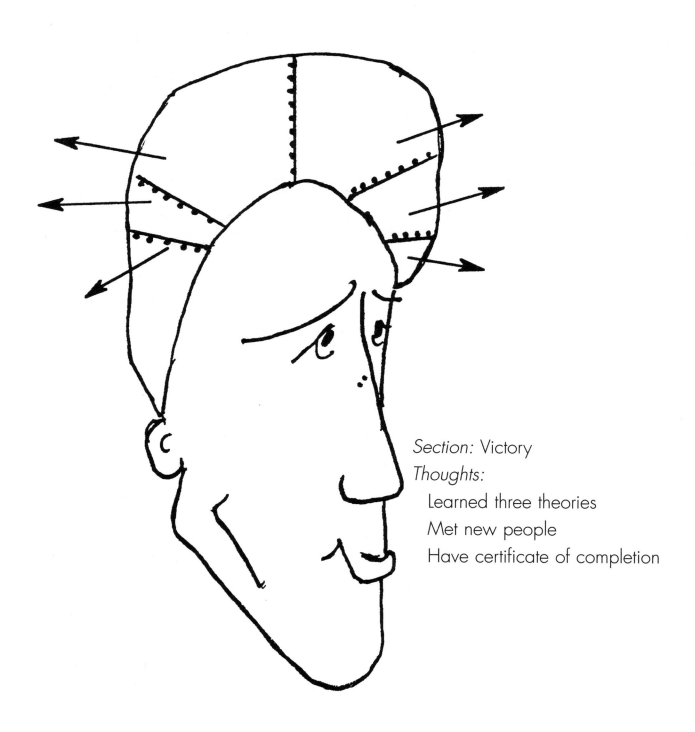

Section: Victory
Thoughts:
  Learned three theories
  Met new people
  Have certificate of completion

81

ARTI-CHOKES

FORM

A great many employees choke at the thought of writing—even when they have to write about something they know quite a bit about. This closer assumes participants have learned quite well the material presented in the training, so well that they can write an article about it. They will work in one of three groups to compose the beginning, middle, or end of the article, using the handout as a guide. The activity will take at least 20 minutes.

FUNCTION

1. Divide the group into three teams. Each team will appoint a liaison who will periodically confer with the other liaisons to ensure a logical flow among the three parts of the article the teams are composing. Assign the beginning, the middle, and the end each to one of the three teams.

2. Distribute Handout 81-1.

3. Allow about 20 minutes for completion of the three sections.

4. Ask the liaisons to read their respective sections so the class can hear the article in its sequential entirety.

5. Make copies, if possible, for each participant.

FOLLOW-UP

Spend a few moments finding a catchy title for the article. Here are a few types of titles that usually attract a reader's eye.

o Plays on words
o References to popular titles
o Rhyming titles
o Titles that ask a question
o Alliterative titles
o Formulaic titles (for example, The 4 P's of Productivity)

Invite a freelance writer to the class to discuss the pro's and con's of article submissions to newspapers or trade journals. He or she can also touch upon the importance of editing. Then once the article *has* been edited, submit it for publication to the organizational newspaper at the very least.

TRANSITION

There are those who feel we do not really know what we know until we write about it. Whether or not you subscribe to this theory, you'll probably agree that the writing process does help us organize and order the information we are constantly absorbing. Even if you have no desire to share your thoughts in a public forum, I hope you will, from time to time, reflect on the knowledge you are picking up and write about how the new knowledge relates to the old.

Save these articles—they reflect relatively new knowledge—and compare it once you return to work to the knowledge you already had on this topic. Keep written records reflecting how this training impacts the way you work and the perceptual insights these reflections yield.

HANDOUT 81-1

Directions: Review the following pointers and include as many of them as are appropriate in the article segment you are writing with your team. In its entirety, the article will essentially summarize what you've learned during this training program. No matter which section you have, spend a few moments thinking about what you've learned. Once your team has a list of at least 20 ideas, start to weave them into a cohesive whole, using these pointers as appropriate.

Introduction:	*Try:*	Using a question.
		Starting with a quotation.
		Putting a number in the opening line.
		Defining a term and then expanding on that definition.
		Including a surprising, perhaps even shocking, fact.
		Giving a preview of what the body will contain.
		Delaying the introduction. Give a string of facts and then tell what they lead to or what they mean.
		Making it clear how the reader will benefit by reading further.
Body:	*Try:*	Establishing a basic theme and subordinating other information to it.
		Organizing the information into major sections, perhaps moving from the most important to the least important or vice versa.
		Providing some how-to information; enumerate the points if you do so.
		Using headlines to separate the basic divisions.
		Connecting the major points via transitions.
		Referring back to the question or quotation that appeared in the opening.
		Giving examples.
		Creating word pictures.
		Including a simple graphic if appropriate.
Conclusion:	*Try:*	Summarizing the body in a sentence or two.
		Referring back to the question or quotation in the opening and giving it a twist of some sort.
		Leaving the reader with a concrete idea he or she can use.
		Making the very last sentence a short and powerful one.
		Playing on vital words.
		Restating the purpose or major points of the article.
		Finishing with an anecdote.
		Using a metaphor that captures the key message of the article.

82

THE LETTERMAN LIST

FORM

With David Letterman's favorite list as the prompt, this closer asks teams of four or five to list, in ascending order of importance, the ten most valuable things they learned from the training program just concluded. Altogether, it will take about 10 minutes for the teams to compile their lists. A spokesperson from each team will identify the top two choices on each team's list.

FUNCTION

1. Assemble teams of four or five participants.

2. Have them determine the ten most valuable things they learned from the training and list those things in ascending order of importance, with 10 starting the least important.

3. A spokesperson from each team will read off choices 1 and 2, explain their importance to the other teams, and then tell how the team intends to use these particular knowledge points, skills, or abilities.

FOLLOW-UP

Ask participants to retain their lists and to note the dates when they make direct and deliberate use of these knowledge points, skills, or abilities in the future. Invite all participants to a class reunion six months hence. Their entry ticket to the party will be the presentation of their dated lists.

TRANSITION

These lists represent how you are valuing the information you have acquired during the time we have spent together in this training program. However, time has a way of altering our priorities. Keep this list with you and, once a month, study it to see if shifts have occurred in priorities. The shifts may be dependent on how and how often the knowledge is used and also on the results derived from its application.

83

INTERNVIEWS

FORM

Teams choose their youngest member as their intern. He or she will be coached by the other members during the time allotted until he or she is as ready as possible for the questions you will ask. Three impartial judges will award points to each team based upon the quality of the answers supplied by their representative intern while you grill him or her. Have token prizes available for the winning intern and the team that supported him or her. You will also need a long list of questions that would typically be used on examinations to determine if and how much students have learned. All told, this exercise will take about 20 minutes.

FUNCTION

1.   Prepare a list of questions based on key learning points throughout the training.

2.   Ask three participants to serve as judges. While the intern teams are working, the judges will review your list, add questions to it, and decide what kinds of answers would earn what kinds of scores.

3.   Form teams of six or seven. Ask each to appoint an intern, e.g., the youngest person in the group. They will then spend the next 10 minutes coaching, drilling, and preparing this person to handle any questions you might ask during the review period.

4.   Next allot 3–5 minutes (depending on the number of teams) for quizzing each intern, using questions based on the list of major points. As you do so, the judges will award points according to their preestablished criteria.

5.   Have the judges announce which intern (and thus, which team) is the winner. Award token prizes.

FOLLOW-UP

Increase the sense of competition and heighten the dramatic intensity by inviting a local reporter and photographer (if only from the company newspaper) to be present for the competition and to record it for posterity.

Distribute the list of questions to all participants as a parting gift and say you will call ten of them in exactly 2 months to see how much they remember. Two months later, make the promised phone calls and ask each of the ten to call another person to ask any question on the list. (Note: Depending on the size of the class, the second ten would then call others.)

TRANSITION

I don't know how many of you have studied cognitive theory, but researchers have found that a little competition is good for the learner's soul. The tension it produces actually helps us be more attuned to the knowledge being conveyed. Personally, I feel too much tension can create just the opposite effect and so I wanted to structure this review as a group-effort examination. The worst may be over, but there is still more to come. I have a few questions I want to raise about your action plans for putting all this knowledge to the best possible use.

84

YOU'S FOR YOU TO USE

FORM
This closer takes about 10 minutes; it has dyads or triads completing a handout that asks for suggestions on how the training might be transferred to the workplace. Larger groups then compile their ideas, the top three of which are shared with the class as a whole.

FUNCTION
1.   Point out that the best way to determine the effectiveness of training is to determine if it is being put to use, if it continues to live after its delivery in the classroom. If participants are discussing the training or implementing the training with others when they return to the workplace, then we know the knowledge presented is being employed.

2.   Distribute Handout 84-1. Allow a moment or two for participants to review it. Then ask them to work with one or two others to complete it.

3.   Have groups merge (up to eight people per combination) and exchange ideas, all the while adding to the possible ways of transporting the training knowledge to a wider venue.

4.   Call on each combined group to present their top three ideas for extending the training possibilities.

FOLLOW-UP
Seek a commitment from participants to follow through on posttraining discussions at least one time, with at least one coworker, employing at least one idea from the handout.

Distribute a typed list of all the ideas to prospective enrollees as a means of increasing interest in the training and the uses to which it can be put.

TRANSITION
Having good ideas and not using them is like having hundred-dollar bills and letting them turn to dust in a vault. You've thought of some remarkably effective ways to derive maximum benefit from the training you have received. Now, it's up to you to take these ideas and run with them. Before we leave today, I hope each of you will select one of these possibilities and pledge to share it with a coworker.

HANDOUT 84-1

Directions: Reflect on the training that you have received. What event, experience, or information comes immediately to mind when you think about the practical use of this new knowledge? What would you tell others about the skills you have developed and the additional data you can add to the base you already have?

Work with one or two others to complete the sentences below. Imagine that you are actually telling a coworker or your supervisor about the benefits of this training. Explain what he or she will be able to *do* with it once the course is completed.

1. You will be able to_____

_____

2. You will have improved your_____

_____

3. You will feel more confident about_____

_____

4. You will discover_____

_____

5. You will learn_____

_____

6. You will be surprised by_____

_____

7. You will find yourself_____

_____

8. You will feel_____

_____

9. You will acquire_____

_____

85

SIT 'N' WIT

FORM

This 5-minute closer asks participants to sit quietly and reflect upon how they have used their wits or added to them as the training program evolved. A few extra minutes are needed for reports. (Note: If possible, play a tape recording of soft music, conducive to thought-gathering.)

FUNCTION

1. Provide some background information about the Minnesota Sit and Spit Club: It has 700 members who are obligated to do one foolish thing a month, such as take part in cherry pit-spitting contests. (For further information, participants can write to the club at 45 North Hill, Mankato, MN 56001.) Explain that while these people sit and do something foolish, you are asking them to sit and think.

2. Ask participants to sit in a relaxed position, to close their eyes if they wish, and to think about all the learning they have acquired, all the work they have done, all the ideas they have explored and skills they have developed during the course.

3. After 5 minutes, have them write a few notes about their thoughts.

4. Call on a few participants at random to share their thoughts.

FOLLOW-UP

Have participants make a list of all the learning-relevant things that can be done while they are sitting. Encourage them to plan posttraining Sit 'n' Wit activities—one a month—for their coworkers. Such activities might include panels, debates, learning lunches, sharing knowledge via e-mail and phone calls, et cetera.

Conduct role plays in which one person plays the part of the supervisor asking how this training benefited the participant. The second person responds using notes made during the sit 'n' wit exercise. Then, the two persons switch roles. (Suggest that participants actually have such a discussion with their supervisors when they return to work.)

TRANSITION

You may have seen the poster that declares, "Sometimes I sit and think and sometimes I just sit." If you are not allotting some time in your day for both of these activities, you are robbing yourself of the reflective time so critical to idea incubation. You are also robbing yourself of relaxing time, so important for stress reduction. Because time in a training program is limited,

I have not really allowed you much time for either. However, now that the training is nearly over, I hope you will plan to build both reflective time and relaxing time into your daily schedules.

86

EDUCATIONAL EQUATIONS

FORM

Author Timothy Gallwey maintains that "performance is equal to potential minus interference." This closer, which will take 5 minutes, has pairs working to come up with a comparable formula reflecting their insights regarding the training that is about to conclude. (Prepare the transparencies and the two quotations in this exercise in advance.)

FUNCTION

1. Ask each participant to work with one other person.

2. Show Transparency 86-1. Briefly discuss the meaning of the quotation and equation. Relate the idea to empowerment, the new style of management, creativity, self-directed work teams, high-performance management, and any other business topic that pertains to your training and their circumstances.

3. Next show Transparency 86-2. Lead a discussion centering on biases that you yourself (and corroborating experts) hold. For example, if you were facilitating a program dealing with problem solving, you could assert your belief that problem-solving skills are the sine qua non of effective leadership, management, and teamwork.

You might illustrate your belief in the importance of such skills by making a strong assertion about the place of these skills in education:

I really think our school curricula should be reorganized around the problem-solving theme, no matter what the discipline. When you think about it, isn't life really a series of problems to be solved? [Pause.] And yet, how many of us have really been trained in the various processes for solving the problems we face on a daily, sometimes on an hourly, basis? In a study of 1,000 executives, Dr. Roger Flax found that their biggest complaint about their subordinates was the lack of problem-solving ability.

4. Ask the dyads to create an equation of their own (using any arithmetic or fractional terms) in relation to the training they have received. They should also write a sentence or two explaining their equation.

5. Call on a few pairs at random to share their equated thoughts.

FOLLOW-UP

Post the equations in a long corridor and invite other employees to vote for the one they like best. After you (or a volunteer) have collected the votes for a week, contact the winning pair and present them with some token prize. (A trophy with "#1" displayed would be ideal.)

On a flip chart, write several sentences that have formulas, leaving out one part of the equation. For example,

"A risk-taking environment plus _____ equals innovation."

Give small groups envelopes in which a number of nouns have been written on small strips of paper. Ask the groups to select the noun they feel best completes the thought, and to explain their selections.

TRANSITION

You've put considerable thought into formulating these equations. Let me commend you for being able to encapsulate important thoughts in a user-friendly way. Big ideas deserve little sentences and you have certainly managed to capture cogent thoughts in an easy-to-remember fashion. Now, here is an equation of my own that I'd like you to carry with you and refer to repeatedly in the days and weeks ahead:

$$T - U = 0$$

Training without use equals nothing.

I'm sure you've heard the phrase, "use it or lose it." To me, it represents what happens to knowledge and ability that are stored in a mental attic. After a while the dust has grown so thick and the stored item so rusty that it is virtually unusable. Don't let that happen with the information you have worked so hard to learn here. Use your training, as soon as you possibly can. Otherwise, you will be left with nothing to show for the time you've spent and the effort you've expended.

$$Per = Po - In$$

"Performance is equal to
potential minus interference."
—Timothy Gallwey

$$E - B = L - P$$

"Education without bias
is like love without passion."
—Soren Kierkegaard

87

PROVE IT!

FORM

In this closer, paired participants will be required to prove they have learned something while attending the training program you have conducted. The proof will be presented on handouts, which you will collect and then use to review major points of the course. About 10 minutes will be needed for completing the handouts and another 10 minutes for review.

FUNCTION

1. Ask participants to work in pairs.

2. Distribute Handout 87-1 and ask participants to demonstrate as many proofs as they can.

3. After 10 minutes, collect the worksheets.

4. Appoint three quizmasters and give each one-third of the collected worksheets.

5. Each quizmaster will take one-third of the remaining participants into his or her group and will begin a review session of about 10 minutes. They will use the worksheets to call on various members of their group at random, saying something like, "Prove to me you've learned something. Give me a proof by numbers."

FOLLOW-UP

Brainstorm with the group at least ten ways they can prove to management they have indeed learned something while attending this training. (Two possible ways are listed in the Transition section.)

Ask participants to work in triads with this assumption: Assume you will soon be appearing on a local (or even a national) show. The interviewer has agreed to ask you only those questions you have submitted in advance. Further assume the topic of the show is Proving That Training Dollars Are Well Spent. What questions (at least six of them) would you like the interviewer to ask you about this particular training?

TRANSITION

Although I require no proof beyond what we've done here with the able help of our quizmasters, some of you may work for people who do require proof that the time you spent on training was time well spent. I'd like to suggest that each of you do one of two things as good-faith gestures:

1. *Type up the most salient information from the course and distribute it to all those within your work unit.*

2. *Take the one concept that was most valuable to you and ask for a few minutes at the next staff meeting in order to present it.*

   Either of these, or comparable efforts, will lead to win–win results: Others will benefit from the expertise you have acquired and you will benefit in many ways, such as increasing the likelihood that you will have an opportunity to attend more training programs in the future.

HANDOUT 87-1

Directions: With both lighthearted and serious references, you will have to prove you have actually learned something in this class. The kind of proof asked for is both broad and specific.

For example, Proof by Illustration can be answered this way: "Time management is a lot like juggling. It means doing several different things at once and involves constant prioritizing. Getting overwhelmed and out of balance means I may drop the balls. I can't juggle 20 balls but I can juggle 5, and knowing the right balls to juggle when is what I've learned about time management."

So, you must comply with the *specific* proof requirements. But...you have *broad* leeway in selecting examples of the proofs.

1. Proof by Numbers (Cite some statistic or other numeric reference to the course.)

   _____

   _____

2. Proof by Reference to FDP (Famous Dead People)

   _____

   _____

3. Proof by Well-Known Formula or Theory

   _____

   _____

4. Proof by Illustration

   _____

   _____

5. Proof by Referral to Costs

   _____

   _____

6. Proof by Demonstration (What can you actually do to show you've learned?)

   _____

   _____

7. Proof by Quotation

   _____

   _____

88

COMMENCEMENT SEEKERS

FORM

Using the 10-C Approach to speech writing, triads will prepare a commencement address that combines the past (the course content they have just studied) and the future (ways they will implement their new knowledge). The speeches can be prepared in about 15 minutes. (Additional time will be needed if you opt to have triads actually deliver their speeches.) Make copies in advance of the handout describing the 10 C's.

FUNCTION

    1.   Distribute Handout 88-1 and allow participants a few quiet moments to read it on their own.

    2.   Next form triads and have participants begin to discuss the points they want to include as they seek to apply the past to the future.

    3.   Suggest they rehearse their deliveries at least once.

    4.   Ask for a volunteer to deliver the commencement address.

FOLLOW-UP

Have teams deliver their prepared speeches and invite various members of management to be part of the audience.

    Contact the best-known college or university in your area and obtain copies of commencement speeches. Obtain permission to use them as a class exercise and then duplicate them for examination by participants. Typically, such speeches are designed to inspire. Since participants seeking to effect change will have to inspire their coworkers to share the enthusiasm they are now feeling themselves, they can employ some of the words and techniques used in these speeches.

TRANSITION

The very word "commencement" implies what is about to happen to you. It is true you are completing an educational process. But, at the very same time, you are beginning another process: that of taking what you've learned into the real world. You are commencing to use knowledge acquired in the recent past for the near future. I will not be part of that effort—just as high school or college professors are no longer part of the graduates' world. And so, I can only hope that I have prepared you sufficiently for the exciting futures that lie before you.

HANDOUT 88-1

Directions: The 10-C Approach to speech writing presents 10 C words to be included—some or all of them—in formal speeches. As you read through them, take a moment to jot down relevant thoughts. Then, as a team, prepare a commencement address for your fellow graduates, who, like you, will soon be seeking ways to apply what they've learned to what they do.

1st "C"	Compliment	What general but sincere statement can you make about those who have attended this training program?

_____

_____

2nd "C"	Citing the Occasion	What references can you make to this end-of-training occasion? What references can be made to what preceded it?

_____

_____

3rd "C"	Commonality	What are things these participants have in common? What have they shared? What similar prospects await them?

_____

_____

4th "C"	Concrete Examples	What illustrations can you make to underscore the importance of the training just completed and the plans for the training yet to be implemented?

_____

_____

5th "C"	Comparison and Contrast	What comparisons and contrasts can you make in reference to the training program and the jobs that await us?

_____

_____

| 6th "C" | Challenge | Acknowledge that it will not be easy for them to implement their ideas and express the hope that they will not shy away from the challenge. |

_____

_____

| 7th "C" | Change | Leaders are not status quo maintainers. They are change agents. What changes would you like to see your listeners undertake? |

_____

_____

| 8th "C" | Confidence | What could you say to inspire your audience by appealing to their pride or to their ability to do what you believe they can do? |

_____

_____

| 9th "C" | Closing | How can you best summarize the points you have made? Could you, for example, use a quotation such as this from *Chorus Line*: "Kiss today goodbye and point me toward tomorrow"? |

_____

_____

| 10th "C" | Call to Action | What is it you want your listeners to actually *do* as a result of hearing your words? |

_____

_____

89

THE POINT IS...

FORM

The major points of the curriculum are listed by participants as you write a master list on a flip chart. Participants then write down the numbers of the items they feel they have learned well enough to teach someone else. Participants indicate by a show of hands if they *have* learned each point well enough to teach it. The items with the fewest votes are retaught. Depending on the complexity of the material to be retaught and the number of participants, this closer can take 15–30 minutes.

FUNCTION

1. Using the flip chart to neatly record the numbered responses, ask participants to review their notes and course materials and to tell you what they feel are the major points of the training that is now concluding. Add your own selections until the list numbers around 25 entries.

2. Ask participants to write down the numbers of those items they feel they have learned well enough to teach someone else.

3. Return to the flip chart now and one by one, ask for a show of hands to indicate which items participants feel they have truly mastered.

4. Intensely review those points with the lowest scores.

FOLLOW-UP

Form teams of four. Ask one person to actually teach a second person a particular concept with which he or she feels comfortable. The remaining two members will critique the first person's performance. The process continues until each person has an opportunity to present a concept or skill.

TRANSITION

You may have heard the maxim, "If you are a teacher, by your pupils you'll be taught." Today, you've taught me that what I've taught you did not sink in as much as I thought it had. So, I have to thank you for bringing to my attention those points which I didn't present as pointedly as I might have. I hope, of course, that I've atoned for my instructional sins by reviewing those points that, it seems, several people did not feel they had mastered. Now that we are about to conclude this training, I hope you feel comfortable with all *the main points—so comfortable that you can teach any of them to anyone.*

90

TRAINING BRAS

Goosebumps author R. L. Stine, whose book sales are nearing the 200 million mark, describes his work as a "literary training bra for Stephen King novels." This closer asks participants, working in small groups, to select (and explain their selection of) an article of clothing for the training they have received and how they will wear it when they return to work. (The clothing and accessory choices are listed on the transparency to be duplicated in advance.) Excluding the sharing of their metaphors, the exercise takes about 5 minutes to complete.

FUNCTION

1. Mention the Stine self-metaphor and explain that participants will make similar comparisons between clothing and training. You may choose to use this example:

> *There are those who feel training is like a scarf. It can be used to keep you warm with knowledge. When you head toward the unknown that is outside your comfort zone, you can use the scarf of training to ward off the cold. There are winds of scorn and rains of negativity that you might be exposed to. The scarf will add a layer of protection against them. You can also use your training scarf in a decorative sense. Not that you would ever show off how much you know. But...you could use your training to complement the body of knowledge you currently possess.*

2. Arrange groups of four or five.

3. Show Transparency 90-1.

4. Ask the teams to select one article from the list and explain, in a metaphorical sense, how it relates to the training.

5. Ask volunteers to share their team's responses.

FOLLOW-UP

Assemble a training wardrobe and hang the various items in it around the classroom the next time training is presented on the same topic. Find an old white shirt, for example, and have participants sign their names with special marking pens, giving their metaphoric use for the training shirt. The same signatured insights would be affixed to various other articles of training clothing (excluding undergarments).

Briefly explore how this training could indeed be a training bra for bigger and better things, things such as a consortium or benchmarking efforts, or further education, writing, or moving into the training field (if only in a limited way). Lead a discussion to consider the forces that would drive such a possibility into the realm of reality and the forces that might be restraining the ideal from becoming real.

TRANSITION

We've heard some creative responses to this challenging assignment. Admittedly, it was done in jest, but I really had an ulterior motive up my sleeve, so to speak. I wanted to have you think about this training from a new perspective, to consider what it can do for you and others. Knowledge possessors, in my opinion, have a special responsibility to use that knowledge in order to make the workplace a better place. You, by virtue of this training, are knowledge possessors. And so, if the shoe fits, wear it!

hat	girdle	coat
shoes	boots	belt
gloves	slippers	wallet
socks	jogging suit	tie
brush	robe	shirt
purse	suit	comb
watch	ring	sweater
t-shirt	slacks	dress
skirt	earrings	bow

91

FRIENDLY PERSUASION

FORM

Working alone or with one other person, participants spend 5 to 10 minutes preparing remarks persuasive enough to convince supervisors to send other employees to the training that is now drawing to a close. The handout of persuasion pointers (duplicated in advance) will assist them in collecting their thoughts.

FUNCTION

1. Give participants the choice of working alone or with one other person.

2. Explain that you would like them to enumerate the reasons why someone should consider taking this training. In other words, how have they grown or what are the benefits derived from the training or what can they now do (what do they now know) that they couldn't do (or did not know) before.

3. Ask them to prepare remarks so convincingly expressed that a given supervisor would be persuaded to send other employees to the same training.

4. Distribute Handout 91-1. Encourage them to study it before beginning their persuasions.

5. Distribute three small sheets of scrap paper to each participant. Then call on one person to make his or her persuasive presentation. When he or she has finished, ask each person to write one word on the scrap paper: "yes" or "no," reflecting their opinions of whether or not the speaker was persuasive. Collect the scraps of paper and hand them to the first speaker.

6. Call on a second person, repeat the voting process, and then do the same with a third volunteer.

FOLLOW-UP

If possible, invite five or six supervisors to the classroom and form groups of participants so that each group has a supervisor sitting with them. Each person in the group will make a pitch to the supervisors, who will make notes on the extent to which they were persuaded and the reasons why they felt as they did. Upon the completion of all participants' persuasive efforts, the supervisors will offer feedback on the presentations.

Ask each participant to work with one other person to complete this declarative assertion: "As a result of this training, I now know (or, I now can)...." The second person offers only two words in response: "Persuade me." The first person then explains one thing that he or she is especially proud of having learned (or having learned how to do). Once the demonstration is over, have the partners reverse roles and repeat the exercise.

TRANSITION

It's been said that success in the current business climate is a question of influence, not authority. Persuading others is a vital communication tool, especially for those who wish to effect organizational change on a small or grand scale. You now have some very persuasive rationales. I sincerely hope you will use them to influence others—your supervisors and your coworkers—to continue adding to corporate knowledge by taking further training.

1. [P]osition your points. In other words, you would not place cost in a primary position but rather in a secondary position, after the benefits have been enumerated.

2. [E]ngage your audience. This means you should not lecture to them but rather hook them with a question, a statistic, a quote, an anecdote, or an answer to the WIFM ("What's in it for me?) question. Hook them, and then reel them in.

3. [R]elate to their concerns. What emotions might be driving their acceptance or rejection of your proposal? Is it fear? If so, what can you say to allay those fears? Is the desire for acceptance a strong one? If so, appeal to that desire by citing the inclusive nature of what you are suggesting.

4. [S]ummon forth the best that is in them. Americans are not afraid to sacrifice, but they need to have a very good reason for doing so. Just think of all the Peace Corps volunteers President Kennedy persuaded to give up the luxuries of their own lives to bring hope to the lives of the less fortunate.

5. [U]nbuckle the belt of conventional thinking. Encourage them to envision the sights so visible in your mind's eye. Show them how to think outside the box and beg them not to return to it.

6. [A]nticipate objections. Have answers ready to overcome the reluctance they may express for not embracing your idea.

7. [D]etermine how you can facilitate the audience's implementation of the change you are proposing. Offer to help out or to speak out in order to form an alliance with the audience and with other audiences they themselves might have to address.

8. [E]mote. Make your enthusiasm contagious. Let them see the sincerity in your eyes; let them hear the excitement in your voice.

92

THOSE WHO CAN...

FORM

As a means of reviewing everything that has been covered by the training session, participants are asked to assume they are revamping the current curriculum. Teams of four or five will evaluate each major component of the course, will decide what to keep, what to eliminate, what to add, what to put in a different place, and will revise the format accordingly. Plan on at least 15 minutes for this closer. (It would be helpful to have flip chart paper available for each team.) Prepare the transparency in advance.

FUNCTION

1. Form teams of four or five.

2. Ask the teams to outline the course as they remember having progressed through it.

3. Once they have the actual sequential outline (and they are free to ask you for assistance), they are to improve upon it. The questions on the transparency will be useful as they work.

4. Arrange for each team to join one other to share their revisions.

5. Collect the revisions and save them for future study.

FOLLOW-UP

Extend this exercise to the workplace processes in which participants engage. Have them outline the sequential steps of the process and then examine whether those steps are in the best possible order, whether each is adding value, whether some should be eliminated, et cetera.

If time permits, ask participants to return to their outlines and ascertain which parts of the course should remain exactly as they are. Ask them to validate the reasons for their selections.

TRANSITION

Those who can, as I'm sure you've heard, do. And those who can't, supposedly teach. A corollary might be, "Those who have taken training, can critique training." While this exercise really served as a way to review what we have covered, it also served to give me some ideas for making the course even better than it is. Your feedback will be very seriously considered and incorporated wherever possible. Thank you.

What would you change about this course?

What would you add?

What would you subtract?

What would you put in a different place?

What would you emphasize more?

What would you emphasize less?

How would you have started this course?

How would you end it?

93

PLOTTERY TICKETS

FORM

This closer requires you to isolate a panel of experts, who will work with you to identify the three most valuable aspects of the course in terms of future use. As you work, the remaining participants, in teams of four or five, will make a list of 25 key points from the training that is drawing to a close. They will then plot among themselves to determine the three most valuable concepts. If their three match the three chosen by the panel of experts, they will win an appropriate prize. The exercise will take 10–15 minutes to complete.

FUNCTION

1.   Select three students to work with you as a panel of experts. Quietly ask them to begin thinking about the elements of the course that were most valuable to the class as a whole.

2.   Quickly form teams of four or five.

3.   Ask the teams to begin listing 25 specific things they learned in this training program.

4.   As they do so, return to the panel of experts and ask in-depth questions to help them make their selection of the three most valuable points. Don't influence that selection, but do raise questions that should be considered as they work.

5.   Return to the teams. Circulate among them as they finish and ask each team to star the three items they collectively feel were most significant.

6.   Ask a spokesperson from each team to share their three selections.

7.   Compare them to those identified by the panel of experts.

8.   Award token prizes to those who have most successfully plotted their choices. You might let them write their own tickets by asking which of three prizes most interests them, for example, getting out earlier than the others, a free soda, or a used book. (Note: It would be fitting to award actual lottery tickets, but make certain to ask first if anyone has any moral opposition to games of chance. If so, do not use the tickets.)

FOLLOW-UP

Take any one of the lists of 25, and begin reviewing in earnest, calling on various participants to tell you more about the items you have pinpointed.

Find someone in the class or in the organization who has artistic ability. Ask him or her to create a cartoon strip based on the three points each team identified. Circulate the cartoon strip widely and reward its creator by taking him or her to lunch!

TRANSITION

No matter which items you identified as the most valuable, those are the most valuable. What matters to you is actually more important than what matters to our panel of experts—no disrespect intended. Take those three items and put them to very good use when you return to work.

94

ZIP 'N' TUCK

FORM

This closer asks participants to reduce the essence of the course to an easy-to-remember condensation, much like Bruce Tuckman's description of the stages through which teams go on their way to synergy (Form-Storm-Norm-Perform). Allow about 15 minutes for teams of four or five to select some aspect of the course and then reduce it to memorable terms, using suggestions on the transparency prepared in advance.

FUNCTION

1. Start with this mini-lecture:

    Zipf's Law of Least Effort, first published by G.K. Zipf in 1949, maintains that the more effort required to express a given word, the less frequent the occurrence of that word in everyday usage. By extension, the more effort it takes to express a given idea, the less likely we are to use or recall that information.

    Here's an example. Countless books and articles have been written about teams and teambuilding. Let's just see, how many of you have ever read a book or article about teams and teambuilding? Or perhaps has taken a course? [Pause for a show of hands. Call on someone to share what he or she re-members.] Typically, we recall very little of what we saw or heard—even though the author carefully selected thousands of words to explain exactly what he or she thought was important.

    Thirty years ago, a man named Bruce Tuckman published his research concerning the way teams operate. He selected a rhyming phrase: Form-Storm-Norm-Perform. You could use each of those four words as a trigger, allowing you to discourse on each stage without having to memorize any particular thoughts. (Similarly, most professional speakers, rather than write down every single word they intend to say, create an out-line of trigger words and speak from it. The results are always more natural than a rehearsed speech.)

    In this training, between my lectures, the words of your fellow learners, the course materials, the videos, et cetera, you have heard or read thousands of words on this topic. Now, I'm going to ask you to do something I call Zip 'n' Tuck in honor of these two researchers. I'm going to ask you to select a con-

cept or a discrete chunk of knowledge that you have learned about in this training. Then, I'm going to ask you to reduce it to an easy-to-remember phrase so that when you tell others about it or when you want to think about it after the class is over, you will be able to call it up quite easily via this technique of condensation.

2.   Form teams of four or five. Ask each to select some instructional segment covered during the training and to "zip 'n' tuck" it using one of the techniques shown on the transparency.

3.   Show Transparency 94-1.

4.   Allow about 15 minutes for the teams to select their concepts and then to create some mnemonic device for remembering it.

5.   Ask each team to share its results.

FOLLOW-UP

Take any one(s) of the condensed products teams have created and use it as a stimulus to share information, examples, statistics, et cetera regarding the topic cited. Write the condensation on the board and elicit further information regarding it.

Collect all the Zipfean pages, lay them next to each other on a flat surface, and advise participants that their price of exit will be to write something on one of the pages other than their own. That something, of course, must expand the condensed term in a relevant way.

TRANSITION

There is simply no way you could remember everything that was said in a course of this length. But, using Zipf's Law, you don't have to. (Ebbinghaus' Law, for your information, says that within a matter of hours, you will have forgotten about 75 percent of what you heard.) Refer to the shortened terms periodically after the course is over. Mentally review the ideas these condensations trigger. To keep the knowledge alive, you should also discuss the ideas with coworkers.

Acronyms (H-O-M-E-S stands for the names of the Great Lakes)

Rhyme (Form-Storm-Norm-Perform)

Alliteration (The C's of Credit)

Numeric reference (Seven Deadly Diseases)

Poem

Winner/Loser list

Short phrase ("It's the economy, stupid.")

95

TOOTH OR CONSEQUENCES

FORM

Via a graphic depicting teeth, participants will be asked a number of questions regarding the training that is drawing to a close. The first team (of four or five) to complete the worksheet will win a tooth-related prize. This closer takes 5–10 minutes to complete. You need to prepare the worksheet and the flip chart notes explained below and purchase tooth-related prizes.

FUNCTION

1. Decide in advance the five most meaty topics or concepts that were presented during the training. Write these on the flip chart but keep the list covered.

2. Ask participants to form teams of four or five.

3. Distribute Handout 95-1 and ask teams to work as quickly as they can to complete it, without reference to any course materials. Uncover the flip chart list.

4. Award inexpensive toothbrushes or tubes of toothpaste or small bottles of mouthwash to the winning team.

5. Ask them (and subsequently each of the other teams) to share the topic they selected and the tooth-points they recalled about it.

FOLLOW-UP

Work with management to create a monthly competition. Determine first what management would like employees to know about the company, about specific product features, about select customers, about how to answer the phone, et cetera. Have the mouth displayed in a public, well-read, or well-traveled location. The person who submits the longest list of related terms or ideas wins. The prizes for the competition could be, for example, free teeth cleaning, a year's worth of dental floss, a water-pic, et cetera.

List some of the terms commonly associated with teeth and encourage teams to get mouthy about them in relation to business practices. For example, using the word *floss*, one might say, "A kind of plaque forms over our creativity if we allow ourselves to become too comfortable with familiar ways of doing things, familiar ways of thinking about things. Training, in a sense, is the floss that allows us to dislodge the layers of old, repeated practices. It removes such plaque so we can keep our minds clean of debris, of extraneous thought, and keep them constantly open and fresh."

TRANSITION

The toothy grin you see me wearing reflects the fun I had watching you work to remember important points from the course. Admittedly, a bit of competition always makes the learning process more enjoyable. When you return to work, though, you will probably not have such competition. So, I encourage you to think of ways you can keep this learning alive and engage in some friendly competition as you do so. You are limited only by your imagination.

Directions: On the flip chart, you will see some of the most critical concepts we have studied. You and your team will select one now that you collectively feel you know quite a bit about. Write your selection here. _____

Now, without looking at any course materials or notes you have taken, fill in one related point on each tooth in the diagram below. This means you and your teammates will have to discuss the concept and then write in specifics—one per tooth on the diagram below. The first team to have a different detail in each tooth will win a prize.

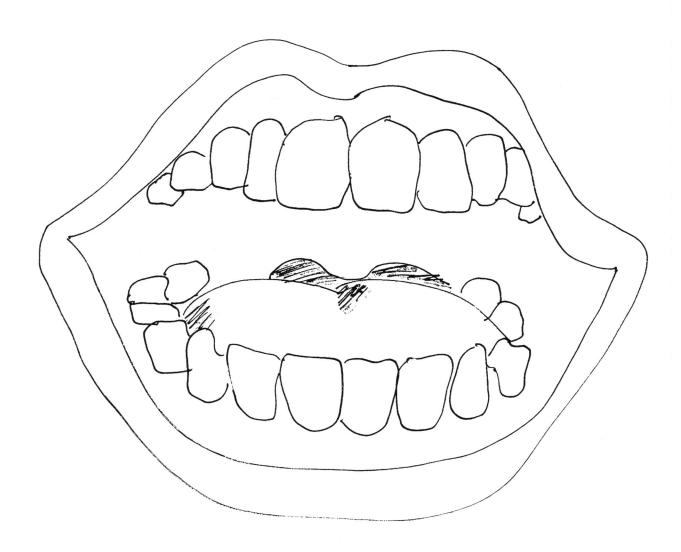

96

HY-FUN

FORM

Working in pairs, participants will try to figure out hyphenated words (shown on a prepared transparency) that relate to business topics. Allow about 10 minutes and determine which team of five or six had the highest number of correct answers. Award a hyphenated token prize, such as a Coca-Cola or a package of Cheez-Its or a Bit-o-Honey candy bar.

FUNCTION

1. Explain this closer as follows:

   I have selected some common business terms that relate, directly or indirectly, to the training we have participated in today. Each of the terms is a hyphenated term such as problem-solving. The challenge is to figure out the words when you are only given part of each. For example, "problem-solving" would be written as "lem-sol." (Note: Show this hyphenated term and its partial representation on the flip chart.)

2. Ask participants to form teams of five or six.

3. Show Transparency 96-1.

4. Allow about 10 minutes for completion before determining which team had the highest number of answers.

5. Award the token prizes.

6. Go over the answers:

1)	decision-making	2)	world-class
3)	re-engineering	4)	mind-set
5)	off-site	6)	e-mail
7)	face-to-face	8)	long-term
9)	self-starter	10)	on-the-job

FOLLOW-UP

Review each of the terms and call on someone to explain how each pertains to the course work they are just completing.

Select terms germane to the topic of the training and prepare a separate worksheet for those.

I certainly hope you consider this exercise time well spent. My purpose in giving it to you was two-fold. I wanted you to have a chance to wind down after all the brain-cramming you've engaged in. But I also wanted you to step back from the intensity, the details of the course itself and think about its relationship to some broader, more abstract terms such as problem-solving. In the weeks and months ahead, try to keep both kinds of knowledge in your head simultaneously—the specifics of the course and the general purposes for having taken it.

1) on-ma

2) ld-cl

3) e-en

4) nd-se

5) ff-si

6) e-m

7) e-to-f

8) ng-te

9) lf-st

10) n-the-j

97

PRESUME TO SUBSUME

In keeping with the cognitive learning theory of subsumption, this closer asks small groups of three or four to review what they have learned thus far and to file it in already established mental storage folders. Depending on what material has been covered, the exercise will take about 15 minutes. It requires one transparency to be prepared ahead of time.

FUNCTION

1.   Introduce the activity this way:

A learning theorist by the name of D. P. Ausubel formulated the subsumption principle to describe how we handle new knowledge, such as the knowledge you have acquired in this training program. He posits that if we can find a logical mental storage folder into which we can place our new file of information, then we will subsequently find that file more efficiently later.

More important than finding it, though, is the recall aspect: We will retain the information in the file for a longer period and will be able to retrieve it more easily. It will make sense to us because it has been related to similar knowledge that we have already acquired. Ausubel asserts that learners should subsume data under mental categories that already exist before beginning to use that data.

For example, if I began talking about Franco Harris, you would quickly open a folder labeled Sports. Within that folder might be a file on NFL Teams. You could place my Franco Harris story with other information once you have established which team file this new information would go in—the Pittsburgh Steelers in this case. You do this very quickly and, with familiar material, you do it without conscious thought. But with new information you have to work more slowly, more deliberately, to ensure the new data are stored in their proper place.

2.   Ask participants to form teams of three or four.

3.   Show Transparency 97-1 and keep it visible for the duration of this closer.

4.   Explain that as a summary exercise, you are going to toss out the names of five main topics covered in depth in this training. After each

has been mentioned, participants will answer the transparency questions regarding it. Then they will confer with their teammates. The actual answers may be different but as long as they are logical, they are acceptable.

5.   Ask for volunteers to share any interesting insights that came to them as a result of comparing their answers with those of their teammates.

FOLLOW-UP
The subsumption process, when done deliberately and with attended thought, does take time. However, the more frequently it is done, the less time it takes. Encourage participants at the beginning of a staff or team meeting and after the topic or purpose has been announced, to ask the leader to allow a few minutes for people to write down what they already know about the topic and then to discuss how the new information could be subsumed in files that are already open (or projects already under way.)

A large display can be mounted in a highly visible place. Organized around a large issue or process, the display will grow as new information is added to it. The subsumed ideas should be written on small cards readily available (along with pencils) to passersby. They will place the cards with their additional thoughts in the proper subsumption category. The insights could be synopses of journal or newspaper articles, for example, related to the display topic.

TRANSITION
Just as there are people who demonstrate precision as they organize their physical possessions, there are people who are that orderly with their mental possesions. They think about the best place to put incoming information rather than just plopping it into their gray matter. They think about large mental folders that may have already been opened in their mental file cabinets. Next, they think about files that are already part of that folder. They decide if the new information belongs in one of the open files or if it should have a new file all its own. This process is done deliberately and the more it is done, the faster it can be done.

Long after this training has concluded, I hope you will use this subsumption principle. As you encounter new knowledge, check to see if you already have some folders started and files within those folders. You've opened many new files as result of this training. Continue to fill them.

Write down all the pertinent points you can recall about this topic.

Into what existing mental folder could you place this information? (Give the name of this folder.)

Is there an existing file in this folder where this information could be placed?

If so, what is the name of that file?

If not, what label would you give to the new file?

98

JUXTAPOSED PAIRS

FORM

This closer involves small groups of five or six, one of whom pulls a pair of words from an envelope and then somehow relates the words to the training topic, for no more than a minute. Each person in the group follows suit. The group then decides which speech they wish to present to the other groups and does so when called upon. The exercise requires about 15 minutes. In advance, you should duplicate the juxtaposed pairs on the handout, one sheet per team, cut them out, and put the pairs into envelopes (one per team).

FUNCTION

1. Explain that this summary exercise is not a typical one. Rather than a mere reiteration of the course content, this review is prompted by two seemingly unrelated words. The word pair must be related to the training in some way. For example, if the two words were *elephant* and *tissue*, the relationship to the training might be made in this way by a classroom participant:

> *I'd like you to imagine an elephant being supported on a thin yard of tissue paper. If you have that image in your mind, then you will know how I felt when I first entered this training room. The enormous weight I was carrying—the burden of doubt, of vanishing confidence, of fear—was bound to rip through the fragile layer of knowledge being offered me. I was certain I would come crashing to the floor when the first question was asked. But I didn't; I was able to answer that question about the supplier chain and the next three questions as well. I remember one was about driving out fear, another about stabilizing processes, and the third question dealt with team leadership. [Supply appropriate terms here.] All of a sudden that tissue paper seemed as strong as marble.*

2. Divide the group into teams of five or six.

3. Give each team an envelope filled with juxtaposed pairs.

4. One at a time, they will withdraw a pair and relate it to the training, as was done with the *elephant* and *tissue* example.

5. When each person has had a chance to deliver the pairs speech, the teams will vote on the one speech they would like to present to the group at large.

6. Have the teams make their presentations.

FOLLOW-UP

As the team speeches are being delivered, ask half the participants to critique them in terms of the training message and the other half to critique them in terms of the training techniques used. Hold a brief session following each speech in which feedback is presented (as diplomatically as possible) to each presenter.

Give participants a parting gift—Handout 97-2, which contains an additional set of juxtaposed pairs. Ideally, they will take one a week and use it to develop their verbal agility by relating the pairs to the training just concluding.

TRANSITION

This exercise required some pretty quick thinking. But such an exercise affords an excellent opportunity to handle the questions that are often asked of us upon our return to the workplace. While there is no way you can possibly anticipate every inquiry every colleague could ask, if you have polished your quick-thinking skills, you will be better equipped to give golden-tongue instead of trip-on-tongue answers. Keep practicing with juxtaposed pairs—they'll turn you into a tongue-fu expert in no time at all!

spider - nail polish

snail - brick

jazz - soap

idea - humiliation

multiplication - ink

stranger - honesty

notion - technology

keyboard - built

land - stapler

sail - daisy

nap - shame

family - dial

gold - corn

struggle - cynicism

misery - thread

addresss - rose

1. aboard - increment

2. Abe - integer

3. adrenaline - imitation

4. adult - illusion

5. buoy - intern

6. bridge - linoleum

7. bullfrog - litigation

8. buffet - limit

9. century - loaf

10. cold - laughter

11. center - manufacturer

12. cough - mannequin

13. department - mobility

14. delirium - manuscript

15. duty - mockery

16. drill - nun

27. peril - jury

28. persuasion - joy

29. phase - jet

30. picnic - jinx

31. pirate - jiggle

32. rags - insomnia

33. ranch - intelligence

34. reality - instrument

35. rationale - mutiny

36. salt - cave

37. sleeve - sky

38. skillet - cloud

39. star - publicity

40. stamina - panel

41. voice - deck

42. volcano - velvet

17. dump - mistake

18. ease - moccasin

19. egg - negotiation

20. excitement - nectarine

21. excavation - nastiness

22. exclamation - needle

23. fitness - oil

24. furniture - opposition

25. flare - onlooker

26. flavor - party

43. virtuoso - hanky

44. volume - haven

45. whale - heap

46. weapon - hay

47. yacht - heart

48. year - software

49. poison - magic

50. marathon - ethics

51. lace - morale

52. yard - beetle

99

GIVING YOU THE RUNAROUND

FORM

This closer works in lieu of an official final exam, requiring participants to "run around" the room, ensuring they have at least basic knowledge of the topics you have listed as the most critical elements of the course. Allow about 10 minutes for their study time and another 10 minutes for the testing time. The only advance preparation is to make a list (and post it on chart paper or on duplicated handouts) of the 10 to 20 elements you feel they should have learned during the training.

FUNCTION

1.   Post the elements of the course you feel everyone should know when he or she leaves the training.

2.   Explain that the final exam will be an oral one. Better still, each person will only have to answer one question related to one of the most vital aspects of the course. (Point to those items on the flip chart now.) Tell them the only problem is that they do not know which question will be theirs.

3.   Now explain they will have 10 full minutes to run around the room and ask others (or you, yourself) to help them remember or relearn each of the points they are not certain of.

4.   Begin the final exam by starting with the first item on the list. Call on one person and ask him or her to fill in the details about this term. When he or she has done so to your satisfaction, move on to the second term. (If the person cannot answer the question, offer an escape by asking, "Would you like to pass?" With gratitude in his or her eyes, the person will probably shout, "Yes." Then ask him or her, "To whom would you like to pass?" Whoever is then named becomes the question answerer.)

FOLLOW-UP

Ask participants to briefly define the terms and then to create a crossword puzzle using them.

Ask for volunteers to form a panel that will discuss (not merely give details about) each of the terms you have identified as essential elements graduates should have mastered.

TRANSITION

We have only taken about ten minutes to review these important terms. If there are some about which you still feel uncertain, I hope you will stay after today or at the very least return to your notes or the course materials to have your questions answered. These are the vital elements of the course. If you have not mastered them, for whatever reason, there is still time to fill in your knowledge gaps.

100

SUMO SUMS

FORM

Based on the awards presented at sumo tournaments, this closer asks groups to think about the various behaviors exhibited by their fellow learners during the course of the training. Then, awards are presented for atypical learning behaviors. You will need about 15 minutes for this exercise. To heighten its effectiveness, have blank award forms available (no more than five per team) for the groups to fill in and then present.

FUNCTION

1. Briefly tell the class about the sumo tournaments in Japan, at which several prizes are given in addition to the prize given to the over-all winner. There is a fighting spirit award, for example, for the wrestler who has demonstrated the most courage.

2. Express your gratitude that the group as a whole has worked so hard. Note that they have earned your respect because of the intensity they have demonstrated and the willingness to explore that they have shown.

3. Acknowledge that they all deserve awards for hard work but that you would like some atypical awards to be given to special participants for the special things they have said and done during the course of the training.

4. Form teams of five or six and distribute five blank awards per team. Ask them to decide who in the class has demonstrated a special or unique behavior and thus should be given an award—like the congeniality and photogenic awards given at beauty contests. Award categories might include friendliness, humor, listening, note taking, et cetera. The awards could be for humorous reasons (bringer of highest-quality doughnuts) or for serious reasons (most likely to explore a difficult question).

5. Ask one person from each team to present the awards to the others in the room. Continue with the presentations by the other teams.

FOLLOW-UP

Hand out sheets of paper to each participant so that in a class with 20 participants, for example, each would receive 19 sheets. Ask one person to stand and the others to write one positive thing they observed or learned about this person. Collect the sheets, hand them to the person standing, ask him or her to be seated and then ask a second person to stand. Continue the process until each person has had feedback from every other person.

Have available Robert Nelson's book, *1001 Ways to Reward Employees*. Hand it to one person and ask him or her to find ten ways, costing less than ten dollars, to reward employees. Ask the person to read his or her list. Then discuss the suitability of these ideas as a means of encouraging coworkers to accept some of the plans resulting from this training program.

TRANSITION

Having survived the course is reward enough for most of you, I am certain. You don't really need any further recognition. And yet, recognition from your peers, even when it is for atypical achievements, is usually deeply appreciated. Keep in mind the way you felt when you received one of these awards or the way you saw the recipients react as they received the awards. Then think about ways you can recognize coworkers when you return to work—especially those coworkers who assist you in implementing the plans you have made to apply this training to your job.

BIBLIOGRAPHY

Armstrong, David. *Managing by Storying Around.* New York: Doubleday, 1992.

Bridges, Bill. *Job Shift.* New York: Addison-Wesley, 1995.

Burrus, Daniel. *Technotrends.* New York: HarperCollins Publishers, 1993.

Butler, Gillian and Tony Hope. *Managing Your Mind.* New York: Oxford University Press, 1995.

Crosby, Philip. *Let's Talk Quality.* New York: McGraw-Hill, 1989.

DePree, Max. *Leadership Is an Art.* New York: Doubleday, 1989.

Dichter, Ernest. *How Hot a Manager Are You?* New York: McGraw-Hill, 1987.

Exner, John. *The Rorschach: A Comprehensive System.* New York: John Wiley & Sons, 1986.

Handy, Charles. *Gods of Management.* New York: Oxford University Press, 1995.

Harary, Keith and Eileen Donohue. *Who Do You Think You Are?* New York: Harper Collins Publishers, 1994.

Kanter, Rosabeth Moss. *World Class.* New York: Simon & Schuster, 1995.

Le Boeuf, Michael. *The World's Greatest Management Principle.* New York: Putnam's, 1985.

Lewin, Marsha. *The Overnight Consultant.* New York: John Wiley & Sons, 1995.

Naisbitt, John and Patricia Aburdene. *Megatrends 2000.* New York: William Morrow & Company, 1990.

Nelson, Robert. *1001 Ways to Reward Employees.* New York: Workman Publishers, 1994.

Peters, Tom. *The Pursuit of Wow!* New York: Random House, 1994

Stack, Jack. *The Great Game of Business.* New York: Doubleday, 1992.

Tannen, Deborah. *Talking from 9 to 5.* New York: William Morrow, 1994.

Trout, Jack. *The New Positioning.* New York: McGraw-Hill, 1997.

About the Author

Dr. Marlene Caroselli is a professional trainer and the bestselling author of six books on training and development topics. She has a doctorate from the University of Rochester.